# WHAT'S YOUR GAME PLAN?

## Creating Business
## Strategies that Work

# WHAT'S YOUR GAME PLAN?

## Creating Business
## Strategies that Work

## MILTON C. LAUENSTEIN

**DOW JONES-IRWIN**
Homewood, Illinois 60430

ISBN 0-87094-593-9
Library of Congress Catalog Card No. 85-71922

Printed in the United States of America

1 2 3 4 5 6 7 8 9 0 D 3 2 1 0 9 8 7 6

# Preface

Like most Americans, I was brought up to believe that private industry was remarkably efficient and that corporations rarely made serious errors. But on my first job, I was soon disillusioned. And in the 37 years since then, I have come to see management miscues as the norm, not the exception. One can hardly open *The Wall Street Journal* without reading about yet another company divesting itself of an activity it clearly should never have undertaken in the first place. Some of these blunders have involved write-offs in the hundreds of millions of dollars. Thousands of smaller enterprises have failed to identify anything they could do particularly well and plod along earning a substandard return on capital, if that.

From the time I first became aware that companies often committed serious errors, I wondered why. I sought to understand what led intelligent executives to go astray. I joined a consulting firm, got an MBA, became a director of long-range planning, taught Business Policy at the University of Chicago, always seeking insights as to why corporations made so many mistakes.

Nearly a quarter-century ago, I became chief executive officer of a small company. In my 14 years running Ventron Corp., I made mistakes of my own. I began to see more clearly some of the problems top management faces. I began to see why the usual approaches to strategic planning have proven to be useless or even counterproductive. In more recent years as a corporate director, consultant, and teacher, I have learned more about how a business can create a game plan that really works.

My objective in writing this book is to help practicing executives avoid some of the errors so many of us tend to make. It is to convey

v

to managers and teachers alike some of the insights I have gained in hopes that it can contribute to American industry becoming more like what we all want it to be.

This volume is quite different from the many textbooks on corporate strategy. It is written not for schools, but for managers. Its suggestions about how to formulate a strategy vary sharply from what is taught in business schools. It reflects practical experience rather than theory. Yet it is also built on a conceptual framework stressing the importance of each company finding and pursuing the unique economic role it can fill best.

For the ideas in this book, I am indebted to a great many individuals. My teachers and colleagues in the Graduate School of Business at the University of Chicago, men such as Sidney Davidson, John Jeuck, George Schultz, and Joel Segal broadened my understanding of management. My directors at Ventron and colleagues on other boards, too numerous now to name, have contributed much of whatever is of value in these pages. Less directly, but no less significantly, people I worked and studied with in engineering school, in the navy, in art school, in graduate school in economics, and in the various companies with which I have been associated have helped shape the perspective from which I view management. More recently, colleagues on the faculty of the College of Business Administration at Northeastern University have provided continuing stimulation, information, and ideas that have influenced what is set down here.

I would like to thank those who participated more directly in producing this volume. Professor Wickham Skinner, Russell Morrison, and Harry Brustlin provided valuable comments and suggestions. I would like to thank my secretary, Val Guilfoy, for her patience in typing draft after draft, month after month, in what seemed like an endless task. Finally, I would like to thank my family for their support and encouragement, for their comments on what I wrote, and above all, for their tolerance and understanding.

# Contents

# PART 1

# DRIVING OR DRIFTING?

# 1

# Setting Your Course

In any competitive activity, fundamentals are important. A football team, for example, needs talented personnel. The players must know how to block and to tackle, how to run and to pass, and how to catch. They must be able to work together as a team to execute their own plays and to stop their opponents.

But the outcome of a particular game is not determined by talent and skills alone. It depends as well on how the team's capabilities are used. Against one opponent, a passing attack may be effective. Against another, a running game may have more promise. The weather may affect what works best. So each coach studies his team's strengths and weaknesses relative to his opponent's and comes up with a strategy. Whether it wins or loses will depend on the relative merits of each team's game plan as well as on its talent and skills.

In business, too, fundamentals are important. A company needs talent. It needs to know how to manufacture and to sell, how to organize, to motivate, and to communicate, how to plan and to control. It needs discipline. It must be able to integrate all of the functions into an effective operating unit.

It also needs a game plan. But unlike the football team, it cannot define a new one every week. A company is in a game which lasts indefinitely. Entering and leaving markets, reallocating resources, reorienting a research effort or a marketing program are enormously expensive. Vacillation leads to failure. To succeed, business must set a course and continue to pursue it aggressively until it has good reason to change. Much more than in football, a game plan in a business must be right.

## GOING YOUR OWN WAY

A key objective of a company's strategy is to position itself so as to enjoy a competitive advantage. That means doing those things it does best and staying away from activities for which others are better equipped. It means filling an economic role for which the firm can become uniquely well qualified. It means steadily building the capabilities and resources needed to excel in carefully defined businesses. It means resisting the pressures and temptations to be misled by short-term considerations, by what others do, or by conventional wisdom. It means having the vision and courage to go one's own way rather than to run with the herd.

Unlike football, business provides an opportunity for each enterprise to define its own game, to select its own playing field according to its own capabilities. A company can choose which markets to serve, which customer needs to fill, and how it will fill them. It is not required to engage in activities in which it is unlikely to excel. It can define its business however it chooses so as to operate in areas in which its talents promise the most attractive returns.

Unfortunately, business executives share a natural human tendency to emulate success. In nearly every industry, most of the participants pattern their approach after that of the industry leader. And often the leader is only continuing to do what worked well for it in the past. For over half a century, Ford and Chrysler have followed General Motors in applying the basic concepts introduced by Alfred Sloan in the 20s. Colgate and Lever Brothers have followed Procter & Gamble, Firestone has followed Goodyear, Westinghouse has followed GE for decades. The best these copycat companies can expect is mediocre results.

By doing the same things in the same ways as their stronger competitors, they confine themselves to dreary competitive treadmills. Their efforts to improve their performance are remarkably similar. They try to develop superior products, to increase productivity, to sell harder, to improve quality, to motivate their employees to greater and greater effort. But they have no real basis for expecting to outperform their competitors. Their approach is epitomized by the Avis slogan, "We try harder". The result is only a struggle to hold their own against ever-increasing pressures on earnings. They sing the sad refrain, "We have to run faster and faster just to stand still."

That, of course, is the nature of a treadmill. No matter how fast you run, you stand still. As long as you are using the same approaches as your competitors, you have no sound basis for expecting to excel. The harder you try, the harder your competitors try. Each of you has ideas about how you will increase your share of the market. But you are playing a zero sum game: For every gain by one entrant, there is a loss by another. And lost business often spurs the loser to claw its way back to regain some of its lost share.

The way to get ahead is not to try to run faster than anyone else. *It is to get off of the treadmill, to set a course of your own.* It is to discover your own unique talents and to do those things for which you are better equipped than anyone else. It is to position yourself so that your customers really need you because no other firm can serve them so well.

In his excellent book *Competitive Strategy* (The Free Press, 1980), Michael Porter provides insights as to what determines the relative profitability of various *strategic groups* within an industry. "A strategic group," he says, "is the group of firms in an industry following the same or a similar strategy." Using the analogy above, he shows that some treadmills are easier to push than others. The book also provides a clue to how to get off of the treadmill altogether when Porter observes, "Each firm could be a different strategic group." By defining a unique economic role for itself, a company can establish a sound basis for expecting success.

The definition of a company's economic role should include both the capabilities and resources in which it will excel and the specific market segments it will address. Which market segments a firm should target depends on what it is best qualified to do. Which capabilities it should develop depends on the market segments it selects. This mutual interdependency is illustrated in Chart 1–1.

Management assesses the company's capabilities relative to its competitors' and selects market segments in which it can reasonably expect to excel. It analyzes the key determinants of success in these segments and establishes a program to develop superior capabilities in these particular areas. This program adds to the firm's distinctive competence to serve the targeted customer groups more effectively than competitors can. By going its own way, it escapes the competitive treadmill. It becomes what Porter calls a

**CHART 1–1**

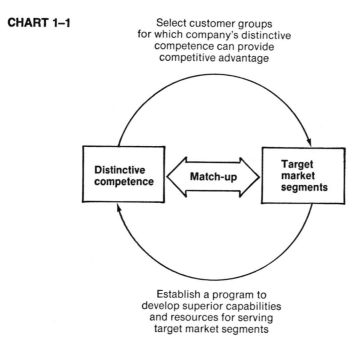

Select customer groups
for which company's distinctive
competence can provide
competitive advantage

Distinctive competence ⟷ Match-up ⟷ Target market segments

Establish a program to
develop superior capabilities
and resources for serving
target market segments

strategic group of its own. It builds a position that can be defended and that can yield attractive returns over a long period of time.

In this way, every business can be a winner! By targeting those specific customer groups for which it is best qualified, and systematically adding to its capabilities to serve those particular markets, any company can do well. To the extent that each enterprise channels its efforts and capital to those areas in which it is best qualified, the economy will be more productive. When companies simply compete head-to-head without any advantage, they have no reason to expect good results. Moreover, such duplication of effort represents economic waste that hurts the economic performance of the whole country.

The validity of this concept has been demonstrated time and again by companies covering the entire range of American industry. For example, after World War II, most automobile manufacturers were trying to outdo each other in the size of the cars they offered. Little American Motors took a different course. It developed a small, practical, fuel-efficient machine it called the Rambler. It was a great success. After a few profitable years, AMC had rebuilt its balance sheet and was the leader in its particular segment of the market.

Unfortunately, this story had an unhappy ending. AMC management apparently attributed its success to an innate ability to outperform its competitors. With its new-found financial strength and with great enthusiasm, it launched a direct attack on GM, Ford, and Chrysler. It developed a full range of cars to compete across the board. It jumped right back onto the competitive treadmill, one on which it lacked the strength of its larger rivals.

Predictably, the result was disaster. AMC plunged back into the red. When it tried to return to its strategy of specializing in smaller cars, it found the going much tougher. By then, the imports had arrived in strength. It was never able to recover the position it abandoned when it tried to become a full-line producer.

In another part of the industry, however, AMC did well over a longer period. It manufactured the Jeep, which for decades dominated its segment of the market. It was consistently profitable. Like the Rambler, it demonstrated that even in the auto industry, a smaller manufacturer that carefully defines its role can succeed.

Recommending that a company go its own way and do its own thing is not at all the same as the conventional wisdom that suggests that specialty products are more profitable than commodities. Neither is it to say that small companies should confine themselves to specialized "niche businesses." In this chapter and later on, we shall see cases in which small companies have done very well in low-margin commodity businesses.

The key issue is the *matchup* between a company's capabilities and the customers' needs. In the long run, it is the company's capability to serve its customers that will determine its success. Capabilities are not general purpose. They apply to the ability to deliver specific products and services to particular groups of customers. The ability to design, manufacture, and market semiconductor chips did not help Texas Instruments in home computers. General Mills' ability to sell foodstuffs did not help it sell Parker games nor Izod Lacoste shirts.

Businessmen would do well to ponder the experience of Ed "Too Tall" Jones, the star lineman of the Dallas Cowboys football team. Because he had size, strength, and agility, he tried to become a professional boxer. But he lacked the requisite skills. He had to return to football, a game for which he was better qualified.

In fact, many capabilities that provide a competitive advantage in one field are actually handicaps in others. An approach to business that emphasizes extensive customer service and meticulous attention to detail is too costly for a commodity business. Wage rates, control systems, marketing concepts, and overhead structure that are appropriate for one industry are completely inappropriate for others. When a company decides to go its own way, it must steer a course consistent with its capabilities, character, and culture.

## BUILDING COMPETITIVE ADVANTAGE

A company's financial results usually depend primarily on the relative strength of its capabilities to serve the market segments in which it chooses to participate. By focusing on carefully defined targets, an enterprise creates an opportunity to build the specific skills and assets needed to succeed there. It may require continuing investment and determined effort over a number of years to achieve a clear, competitive edge. Once achieved, however, it can have a decisive effect on results achieved.

Focusing on an appropriate target can yield outstanding results even in a highly unfavorable industrial climate. It can enable a small company to outperform much larger ones. Two examples from the metals industry illustrate how businesses can succeed in a tough environment by building outstanding strength to serve well-defined market segments.

In the United States, there are over a dozen brass mills. They extrude a variety of shapes made of different copper-containing alloys. These extrusions are used as raw materials for screw machines and for other purposes by a wide range of customers. The industry has been characterized by stagnation, over-capacity, and poor profitability. For many years, each of the mills offered a broad product line, running from standard shapes to specials, in a number of different alloys.

Some years ago, one of the producers, Chase Brass, decided to get off of the competitive treadmill and to go its own way. It elected to specialize in standard, high-volume products and to abandon the rest of the market to its competitors. It limited itself to the single most popular alloy and to only a few standard shapes.

By giving up its ability to make other alloys and shapes, it was able to design its plant to be more efficient in producing standards. Selling a limited product line to fewer, higher-volume accounts simplified marketing. Soon Chase had substantial cost advantages in nearly every aspect of its business, from inventory expense to run length to marketing. By pricing lower, it was able not only to gain marketing leadership but to induce additional users to switch to standard products. It became not only the largest but by far the most profitable brass mill.

Some of Chase's competitors abandoned the business. Others groped for a way to compete profitably in standards while continuing to offer specials. But it was a case of "mission impossible": there was no way they could do both. They felt that they could not afford to lose what volume in standards that they still had. Yet their cost structure made it impossible for them to make any money on them. So they continue to plod along on their treadmills.

Even in the steel industry, building a capability to excel in a well-defined segment has paid off for a number of companies. One of these is Nucor Corp. It targeted the market for steel bars and joists. Initially, Big Steel scoffed at this tiny challenger. But Nucor developed the specialized capabilities to serve that particular market segment better than anyone else. It built highly efficient mini-mills based on melting scrap iron in electric furnaces. It located its facilities in such out-of-the-way places as South Carolina, Nebraska, and Utah. It adopted highly effective employee relations programs. Over a period of 15 years, it grew at a compound annual rate of over 20 percent and built sales volume to over $500,000,000 annually. It averaged over 20 percent on shareholder equity. In 1984, it was one of the 100 most profitable of *Forbes* magazine's list of America's top 1,000 companies.

In a sense, these could be called "niche businesses." But the products are not high-priced specials. They are low-priced commodity items. What Chase and Nucor did that was unusual was to define their businesses in specific terms and to build unique capabilities to serve the particular market segments they had targeted. They did not follow what others were doing. Instead, they had the courage to go their own way. As a result, they were dramatically more successful than others in their industries.

When a company has built a competitive advantage and attained a leadership position in its specific markets, it has an excellent opportunity to expand its resource development program and to extend its competitive advantage. It can exploit economies of scale. It can build its understanding of the market. It can refine its technology and procedures geared to this specific customer group. It can entrench itself in its area as Eastman Kodak did in color film, Procter & Gamble did in soaps, GM did in automobiles, and IBM did in computers. These companies were able to perpetuate their leadership positions for decades.

Unfortunately, as a leader it is psychologically difficult to maintain a determined effort to develop more and more capability to serve customers better. Complacency sets in. Companies become wedded to the approaches that brought them success and fail to adjust to a changing environment. That was the fate of the American steel industry which once led the world.

A quarter of a century ago, it became apparent that new technology and new facilities would be needed to be competitive in the world market for steel. The mills on which the dominance of the American steel producers had been built would no longer be adequate. Future success would depend on larger facilities located on deep water harbors and using the basic oxygen process and continuous casting.

The American companies, being the largest, had the advantage. They had the financial resources to support research and to build the plants. They were in a position to know their markets best. But they clung to the technologies and approaches of the past. So they lost out.

Companies in nearly every major steel-producing country saw the need and erected modern facilities. Not only in Japan but in other Asian countries, in Europe, and even in Brazil, steel producers invested in such mills. Only in America did the industry fail to build new facilities.

The problem was not a lack of capital. Over a period of two decades, when Japan was building its modern capacity, the American steel industry outspent the Japanese by 20 percent. Refusing to recognize the need for new facilities, the U.S. producers squandered their money trying to update their old mills piecemeal. Many of the plants which they tried to refurbish were subsequently shut down, and the investment had to be written off. Now, the United States is no longer able to compete. Foreigners can supply better steel at lower cost even in the domestic market. Unable to make a profit with their old facilities and now unable to finance new ones, the American integrated steel producers have become dependencies of the U.S. government.

General Motors has courted a similar fate. That company was so successful for so long that it relaxed its efforts to improve its capabilities to serve its markets. Only after imports took a significant share of its business did it begin to realize that its capabilities were no longer superior. Finally, in 1984, it launched its ambitious Saturn car project to rethink its whole business and to come up with dramatic new approaches to building automobiles. Had it been more aggressive over the years, it would be in a far stronger position today.

## RUNNING AMOK

The American business community is obsessed with growth. "If you are not moving ahead, you are falling behind," they say. Simply doing an outstanding job of satisfying customer needs and earning a superior return on investment is not enough. To be considered a success, a company must expand.

Senior executives are ambitious individuals. They strive for achievements which will be considered praiseworthy by their peers and colleagues. Many have been dissatisfied with the competitive treadmills on which their companies have been plodding away. But instead of focusing on areas in which they could reasonably aspire to leadership, they have run amok. They have gone on acquisition binges and have diversified mindlessly. They have plunged into businesses which they did not understand and could not manage. In the end, they have lost enormous sums of money. This gross misallocation of capital has been a significant drag on the American economy.

Beatrice Foods, for example, had to admit that it was unable to generate an adequate return on some 50 different businesses it had entered. When it decided to discontinue them, it had to write off $280 million. Similarly Gulf & Western wrote off $470 million when it decided to sell operations it had acquired. Warner Communications' venture in electronic games lost $539 million in just one year and then occasioned a $425 million write-off when the company discontinued the operation. ARCO and Texas Instruments suffered losses of over $500 million each in unsuccessful forays into industries outside their areas of competence.

These enormous debacles are only the tip of the iceberg. Thousands of companies continue year after year to invest in businesses that they are ill-equipped to manage and that produce poor results. A list of over 20 of these dismal situations that happened to be reported in the business press is contained in the box beginning on page 25, Chapter 2.

Companies on the competitive treadmill are not the only ones that participate in this wild game. Businesses that are doing very well in their own areas also fall victim to the siren song of growth through diversification. They fail to realize that the basis for their success has been their special expertise and capabilities in the businesses in which they have specialized. Sometimes, they fail to understand the differences in requirements for success in different parts of the same industry.

The example of American Motors, which attained success with the Rambler and the Jeep but failed as a broad-line automobile producer, has already been cited. Successful regional airlines have been particularly vulnerable to this kind of error. They concluded from their fine performance in the minors that they were qualified to compete in the big leagues. One after another failed in the attempt.

The case of Frontier Airlines is typical. It had been earning over 20 percent on equity as a feeder airline operating out of Denver. Then in 1981, it decided to challenge the major carriers on trunk lines to the West Coast. It discontinued service to 41 smaller cities. Soon it was losing money. It was in a different business, one in which it was not qualified.

To try to return the company to profitability, the CEO adopted a three-point strategy:

1. He initiated a stringent cost-cutting program.
2. He tripled the advertising budget.
3. He announced plans to diversify outside the airline industry.

None of these initiatives addressed the underlying problem. Frontier's capabilities did not match the needs of the trunk line business. It was not equipped to compete there. It was at a fundamental competitive disadvantage. It was in a football game wearing a tennis outfit. By 1984, it was on the verge of collapse.

A more ironic case in the same industry occurred years earlier. Northeast Airlines had been a successful regional carrier. It eyed the heavy traffic to the South and managed to win "temporary" permission to fly to Florida. For years it succeeded in a desperate fight in the courts to retain its opportunity to compete with Eastern and Pan American in a market for which it was poorly equipped. In its success in its battle to keep its trunk lines, it lost the war. It became so weak it had to be taken over by Delta.

## VISION AND CHARACTER

Operating executives, especially those who have come up through the ranks, find it extremely difficult to think broadly about the economic role of a company. Their training and experience and powerful pressures in their current job situations rivet their attention to operating problems. They are consumed by the need to meet current profit targets. They are psychologically chained to the competitive treadmill and are programmed only to pump harder.

The American spirit relishes competition. We approach business as we do an athletic contest in which the objective is to surpass our rivals. We are entranced by the drama of head-to-head competition, of confrontation at high noon. Going our own way and abandoning much of the field to competitors is usually outside of our field of vision.

We are obsessed with growth. Even in an economy that is expanding at only a few percent per year, we cannot accept an objective less than 10 or 20 percent annual sales increase. We choose mindless diversification rather than accepting the challenge of achieving steady improvement in efficiency in a stable industry.

Top management is subject to enormous pressures to produce attractive current profits. The quarterly earnings statement has become a fixation—anything, including the integrity of our accounting, is sacrificed to it. The focus on current earnings pervades the entire operation: It is small wonder that after 20 or 30 years in such an environment, senior executives have trouble giving much weight to basic strategic considerations. They concentrate on doing things right rather than determining the right things to do.

A manager is continually beset by operating problems. Crises in sales, manufacturing, and employee relations arise constantly. The competitor cuts price or introduces a new product. Government regulatory agencies descend on the company. A takeover is threatened. Managers' universal complaint is that they cannot find time to think, to plan, to deal with the questions that will determine the success of their companies in the long term.

On long-term issues, top management thinking is poisoned by the conventional wisdom. Doing what is generally accepted is safer than going off on one's own and trying to be unique. Executives base their decisions on the accepted notions that growth is essential, diversification is good, and modeling one's operations after those of successful companies is smart. They are pressured to carry a full line, to enter emerging growth industries.

The result is that executive vision is impaired. Managers overlook serious risks and major opportunities. They fail to see basic issues about what capabilities to develop. Their blinders focus their attention on the problem of the moment.

The same influences that impair vision undermine executive character. The tyranny of the financial community's fascination with current earnings induces managers to mortgage their future. As executives in the steel industry did, they temporize. They fail to make the investments they know are needed. They make concessions to labor they will not be able to afford in the future in order to avoid a work stoppage today. They puff their companies in financial reports and in presentations to analysts. They take liberties with accounting procedures. They look for shortcuts to enhancing earnings such as acquisition arithmetic or greenmail. They turn to the government for tax relief, protection from foreign competition, or outright subsidies rather than find sounder economic roles for their firms.

Ultimately, many senior executives adopt a simple philosophy of opportunism. They enjoy the freedom to pursue whatever looks good at the moment. They talk about strategy and rationalize their actions with high-sounding allusions to strategic plans. But what they really do is pursue whatever opportunities come into view with little notion of their long-term implications. The results for companies and for the economy are tragic.

Because so few executives are able to develop vision and character in the usual corporate environment, some firms choose leaders who have a different background. Many chief executives were formerly lawyers, investors, consultants, entrepreneurs, or members of owning families, where they developed a broad view of business. These roles foster objectivity and a concern for long-term economic performance, rather than preoccupation with operational details.

Managers who aspire to leadership roles should work to broaden their vision. It is not inborn. It is a talent that can be acquired. One can learn from other executives, from books, and from courses and seminars. One can learn by observing and analyzing what goes on in the business world. One can pursue a career that includes both staff and line assignments, or better still, a stint with an outside service firm in consulting, auditing, or the law. The key is to see the need. If one works to develop his vision, to see what is basic and what is superficial, to understand what leads to superior earnings over the long term, chances are he will succeed.

Senior executives have access to a special source of objectivity and experience to enhance their vision: the board of directors. All of us have blind spots, especially in cases where we are in the middle of a situation. Independent directors with widely varying experiences are in a much better position to see the strengths and weaknesses of a company's position. By drawing on the wisdom of the directors, top management has an opportunity to see situations more clearly and to develop their own vision.

Better vision can contribute to character. When one sees more clearly the implications of a decision, he is better able to resist the temptation to be guided by short-term considerations. He will find it easier to reject the acquisition prospect that may add to this year's earnings and to next year's problems. When he sees that the puffery that gets good press today jeopardizes tomorrow's credibility, he will present a more realistic picture of his company's prospects. When he sees that going his own way can enable him to get off of the competitive treadmill, he will have more courage to strike out on his own, to innovate, to lead.

## PROCEDURES

Most companies with any pretension to being well managed have established procedures for strategic planning. The results have been disappointing—so much so, in fact, that many companies have scaled back their long-range planning programs. Some have abandoned them altogether.

The basic problem in many of these cases has been that top management lacked a clear idea of what strategy and planning were all about. The procedures were designed and led by staff executives who had only the vaguest notion as to how these annual exercises could be translated into practical results. Line managers found them to be a painful waste of time. And, as we shall see, many of these procedures do in fact turn out to be counterproductive.

The key to effective strategic management is a clear understanding of how it can work to make an enterprise more effective and more profitable. When the chief executive sees the big picture, he may be able to lead his firm to outstanding success with no formal strategic planning procedures at all. But if he is totally preoccupied with current problems, annual strategic planning exercises, no matter how sophisticated, are useless baggage.

Formal procedures are likely to be helpful only when management sees clearly the need to set a basic course for its company. Systematically exploring alternative directions can help to define a business so as to get best results. Articulating a clear business strategy can help to coordinate decisions throughout the organization to pursue appropriate goals and to build competitive advantages. Effective long-range planning can help to identify risks and opportunities and to elucidate the most rewarding courses of action.

This book describes procedures for better strategic management. But the reader should remember that procedures are only convenient devices for getting work done. Unless management has a clear idea of the purpose of work, procedures will be empty charades. Until management sees the need for a meaninful game plan, it is pointless to try to establish strategic planning procedures. For a management that is dedicated to preserving its freedom to follow a philosophy of opportunism, planning procedures only get in the way.

We shall now turn to examining in some detail the pressures and influences that make it so difficult for a manager to develop a broad strategic perspective. We shall then discuss executive vision and the role of the board in helping top management set a rewarding course for a corporation. Only after dealing with the central problem of seeing the broad picture will we get into the specifics of strategic planning: defining the business, formulating a strategy, planning for the long term, and establishing financial policies. We shall consider the application of these approaches to different types of businesses: small companies, mature industries, high-tech business, diversified corporations, and service firms. Finally, we shall examine briefly the challenge of implementing the game plan once it is established.

# 2

# Management Myopia

Few would disagree that a well-considered game plan is important to the long-term success of a corporation. Why then do so many companies make strategic errors? Why do companies enter businesses for which they are not qualified? Why does a well-managed enterprise like Texas Instruments lose the better part of a billion dollars in home computers? Why does the once-dominant U.S. steel industry fall hopelessly behind the rest of the world? Are such errors avoidable? Does it take the business equivalent of an Einstein or a da Vinci to see the future? Are we condemned forever to pay the cost of widespread misallocation of capital represented by companies trying to do things that can better be done by others?

One thesis of this book is that ordinary human beings are perfectly capable of seeing ahead. The management of Chase Brass were not geniuses. It didn't take an IQ of 160 for McDonald's to see the opportunities in fast foods. IBM didn't need divine inspiration to realize that it had an opportunity in personal computers. The primary requirement for seeing what to do is simply to look, to commit to understanding the basic economic realities that apply in a business situation.

Even the most prescient executive cannot forecast the future perfectly, see every opportunity and pitfall, or avoid all errors. But a great many colossal blunders could be averted if management would just ponder questions such as:

- Does anyone really need us in this market? Are we honestly making a valuable economic contribution?

17

- Have we identified those capabilities and resources most critical to success in the businesses we are addressing?
- How do our capabilities compare with those of our competitors? Can we expect to develop and maintain superior qualifications over the long run?
- Are there some segments of this industry for which we are well equipped and others for which we are not?
- Have we defined our business so that we invest only in activities for which we are clearly the best-qualified supplier?

These questions apply both to the businesses in which a company is already active and to new ones it is considering.

If an executive will apply himself to answering such questions rigorously and objectively, he will gain valuable new perspectives on his business. He will be less likely to pour money and effort into operations in which he has no basis for expecting success. He will avoid exposing his company to the vulnerability that comes with trying to be all things to all people in his industry. He will identify those specific opportunities for which his company is best qualified and that offer it the greatest rewards.

The problem is that most executives cannot or will not look They suffer from *management myopia* which clouds the vision and makes it impossible to see the long-term implications of corporate actions and policies.

It is management myopia that explains how a company like U.S. Steel could decline so far from its onetime position as America's largest corporation. Its executives failed to see the need for the kind of modern mill needed to be competitive in the world market. They failed to recognize how the American minimills could be so much more efficient than they were. They failed to answer basic questions such as those listed above when they outbid all others to buy Marathon Oil Co. for $6 billion.

The reason they failed was not that these issues were not apparent at the time. Companies in virtually every other major steel-producing country saw the need and built modern mills. Smaller American companies saw the advantages of the minimill approach. Other bidders and the financial community saw that U.S. Steel paid too much for Marathon and was not well qualified to run an oil company. U.S. Steel failed to see these things not because they were so obscure but because it failed to look. It suffered from management myopia.

Management myopia is so common that its absence is often mistaken for brilliance. Consider, for example, Alfred Sloan, one of the most famous American industrialists. His policies enabled GM to take the leadership in the automobile industry from Ford over 50 years ago and to hold it ever since. What was his vision that led to such dramatic results?

Before Sloan, GM was an uncoordinated hodgepodge of automobile manufacturers that it had acquired. They competed directly with one another. No attempt was being made to rationalize production, to take advantage of GM's potential economies of scale.

Ford was at the opposite extreme. Its approach was absolute standardization with no consideration given to differences in customer preferences. The Model T came only in black.

Sloan's vision was simply that customers wanted a choice— but at a competitive cost. So he organized the line systematically according to price and quality, streamlining operations and eliminating a number of brands. By catering to customer needs economically, GM became the industry leader.

For this, Sloan is known as a business genius. It would seem more remarkable that others didn't have the same insight, if it were not for management myopia. This disease is so pervasive that when an executive sees clearly his corporation's opportunities and exploits them, he stands out.

Management myopia is not congenital. It is an occupational disease. It comes from years of working in the trenches, where increasing sales and reducing costs in the short run dominate the thinking. The attitudes and outlook characterized by management myopia are taught to young executives in business schools, in seminars, and on the job. The disease infects the priorities of top management and is transmitted on down the corporate ladder.

Because of the virulence of this malady and its potency in destroying executives' ability to see, we shall examine it in some detail. We shall look at its origins and how the corporate environment nurtures it until it has become epidemic in the business community. We shall consider how it affects the decision-making process and financial results. By understanding it, we shall be in a better position to treat it.

## CAUSES

Our industrial system breeds the management myopia virus. Business schools divide the curriculum into courses and divide courses

---

### CAUSES OF MANAGEMENT MYOPIA

Obsession with growth.

Pressure for current earnings.

Years of experience focusing on narrow problems.

Reward system tied to current performance.

Effect of incremental sales.

Preoccupation with beating the competition.

Presumed effects of superficial appearances on stock price.

Fragmented approach to teaching business.

Emphasis on effort and motivation as cure-alls.

Lure of diversification.

Reliance on conventional wisdom.

Narrow career paths.

---

into topics so that students are taught to deal with fragments of a subject, one at a time. Even the usual capstone course, Business Policy, is seen as bringing together the separate topics previously taught rather than focusing on the concept of the central economic role of an enterprise. We have already seen how the business environment leads to an obsession with growth. Industrial organizations focus their attention on progress in quarterly earnings. Rewards and punishment are tied to current results. If a malign conspiracy were to undertake to prevent the development of vision in executives, it would be hard-pressed to devise a more effective system for fostering management myopia than the one we already have.

The system forces executives to give first priority to operations. Unless an organization can execute effective, strategy is useless. Effective execution is not easy. Assembling the needed resources, organizing them into an integrated program, securing the enthusiastic cooperation of the people who must make it work, and identifying and avoiding pitfalls are challenging tasks. A myriad of current operating problems preempts executives' time. It is not surprising that they are often too busy to ponder their proper economic roles.

Pressures on executives at all levels rivet their attention to their immediate problems. "It is hard to remember that your job is to drain the swamp when you're up to your ass in alligators."

Top management must be sensitive to how quarterly earnings compare with previous periods. It is the dominant factor affecting the price of the company's stock. The financial community *talks* about quality of management and strategic planning, but it *acts* on the quarterly financial statement. Despite the vaunted research activities of investment firms, they are unable to evaluate the potential return from what companies are investing in their futures. As a result, they are limited to relying on current earnings trends. For example, Value Line Investment Survey, the large financial advisory service, rates stocks for its clients every week and explains changes in its ratings. Week after week, *every one* of these changes is based on reported or expected quarterly earnings.

The price of a company's shares is of vital concern to senior executives. Stock in the corporation and options to buy more frequently represent the bulk of their net worth. A drop in its price can have a drastic effect on their personal financial situations. The price of a company's shares affects the prestige of its officers. Moreover, a company whose stock is cheap is a tempting target for corporate predators. When the price of a company's shares falls, managers begin worrying about being taken over and losing their jobs.

The evaluation of any corporation by the financial community affects its ability to raise money and to grow. Poor current earnings can frustrate management's fondest ambitions to expand.

From top to bottom, the system of rewards and punishments is tied to current earnings. For senior executives of large corporations, a good year can yield $1 million or more. Middle managers have an opportunity to earn substantial incentive payments based on the results they obtain in a period of 12 months or less. Sales bonuses are often tied to business generated in a quarter, a month, or as a percentage of sales as they are made.

In addition to their effect on incentive compensation, short-term factors determine executives' base pay and career progress. Salary adjustments are normally made annually and reflect results obtained since the last increase. Promotions are usually based on performance during the last year or two. Ambitious, fast-track executives never expect to spend more than two or three years in the same position. They gear their efforts to that time frame. Results after they have left a job are not relevant to their advancement. If profits decline later, so much the better. It makes it look as if they were abler than their successors.

Short-term earnings variations depend largely on sales volume and on expense control. So management focuses its attention on getting orders and on cutting costs.

Companies apply enormous effort to increasing volume. They struggle to come up with catchy advertising campaigns, sales promotions, or product improvements to boost sales. They spend large amounts of time and money seeking to hire, train, and motivate people who can get more orders.

The most obvious way to increase volume is to take business away from competitors. Executives become engrossed in a competitive chess game. They seek to outthink and outhustle their rivals. They closely monitor what competitors are doing, determined to respond quickly and effectively to any threat. They overlook the possibility of going their own way, setting their own course, defining their business differently from others in the industry. They are on a competitive treadmill.

The crudest competitive weapon is price. In order to lower price without hurting current earnings, a company must reduce its costs. So there is a never-ending campaign to get costs down, to get ahead of competition, or at least not to fall behind.

From the time he enters the industrial milieu, the young executive is immersed in this continual struggle to sell more, to cut costs, to beat the competition. He becomes an integral part of a machine, the objective of which is narrowly defined as increasing current earnings. At first he is assigned simple tasks. Later, he becomes a boss and has more complex assignments. But until he reaches the top, he is concerned not with defining the business but with running it. The desperate struggle to improve current earnings leads to more and more intensive focus on short-term operating problems.

When a person finally becomes a chief executive officer, he typically has spent a quarter-century or so in the competitive rat-race. He has learned that success comes from the intensity and quality of management effort. He is comfortable dealing with people and handling operating problems. He is an expert in making things happen, not in seeing the big picture. His attention is focused on the quarterly earnings statement. He has management myopia.

Some chief executives fall victim to a special strain of the disease called acquisition fever. Having reached the top rung of their corporate ladder, they look for new worlds to conquer. I know from having done it that spending millions to buy companies can be an exhilarating experience. It brings a special sense of excitement and a feeling of power. It is fun! But as one becomes enmeshed in the very special world of buying and selling businesses, he can easily lose track of how his corporation fits into the economy. The definition of the business, if there ever was one, becomes blurred beyond recognition.

Without a vision of a sound economic role for his firm, how does the CEO with management myopia decide what his company should be doing? He relies on what has succeeded for him in the past. He emulates others. He draws on conventional wisdom. He pursues courses of action which can only be expected to lead to poor results over the long haul.

## FLYING BLIND

A company without a strategy is flying blind. The CEO is like the airplane pilot in the bad news, good news story. "The bad news," he announced to his passengers, "is that we don't know where we are nor which direction we are headed. The good news is that we are making excellent speed in getting there."

Without a clear concept of where it is headed, top management adopts an opportunistic approach. It pursues growth wherever it appears to be available: new customers, new products, new markets, acquisitions, diversification—whatever looks good at the moment. It fails to establish any consistent, coordinated program to develop a combination of resources and capabilities that will provide long-term competitive advantage. Without a basic position of strength, it can only grind away on the treadmill, hoping to pump hard enough to get ahead.

An executive naturally bases decisions on what he has found useful in the past. But usually his experience has dealt with operational rather than strategic issues. Considerations that guided him well when he was deciding *how* to do something can be misleading when he must choose *what* to do. For example, he has learned well how much sales volume helps earnings—in the short run. So growth has become a primary goal, an obsession. He exhorts his people to sell harder, to develop new products, to enter new markets, to seek acquisitions, to do whatever will increase sales.

Such thinking leads to participation in activities in which a company is not well qualified. Initially the incremental revenue may add to earnings. But in the long run, all costs are variable. The so-called fixed expenses must inevitably be increased to take care of the additional volume. To the extent that new products and markets are involved and operations become more complex, overhead expenses eventually rise more than proportionally with sales. The new businesses, in which competitors have advantages, are less profitable and grow more slowly than the old. They become a drag.

Ultimately, the company becomes the subject for a news item such as those cited in the box beginning on page 25. A new chief executive recognizes that the new operations are counterproductive, gets rid of them, and finds other areas of his own in which to diversify. The new CEO of Beatrice Foods, for example, had not yet completed his program to divest the mistakes of his predecessor when he bought a whole new bag of problems in Esmark, Inc.

Past experience can also be misleading when it comes to developing resources and capabilities. The American steel industry "knew" it could depend on the facilities that had generated enormous profits in the past. Henry Ford "knew" that rigid standardization was the key to success in making automobiles.

The way in which successful past experience can cause management myopia was demonstrated dramatically, if inadvertently, in a speech made by a top officer of one of America's largest railroads. He pointed out how successful the railroads once had been. Then along came the automobile, the airplane, government regulation, and militant unions to cause problems for the railroads. His company, he said, was the same fine institution it had always been, following the same proven policies that had brought it success in the past. "When, oh when," he asked, "would the rest of the world get back into step with them, so that the railroads could shine again?"

Without having set a clear course for their own company, executives are reduced to looking at what others are doing as a guide for their own actions. When a book appeared identifying the companies and characteristics most worthy of emulation, managers flocked to the bookstores to buy it in record numbers.

Outstanding companies have not achieved their success by copying others. They have developed a distinctive competence of their own which enabled them to create a unique position for themselves. They have seen new and better ways to fill customers' needs and have had the courage to innovate, to lead the way. As any racing sailor knows, following the leader is poor strategy. You split tacks, seeking different winds and currents, to gain an advantage.

As in sailing, following the leader holds little promise for success in business. The number one firm normally has the edge in economies of scale, in reputation, in what it can spend to widen

## FLYING BLIND

A sampling of news items appearing during a six-month period in 1983.

May 23, 1983, *Business Week*
"Kennecott Corp. took over Carborundum Co. in 1977.

"But the prize turned into a pratfall. When Kennecott purchased it, nearly half of the Carborundum's sales and earnings came from abrasives. On April 28, Sohio announced it was taking a $75 million after-tax write-off to shut or sell most of that business. And this decision followed the divestiture of other Carborundum businesses ranging from environmental systems to camshafts.

". . . a growing number of senior Carborundum executives left. . . . Kennecott's managers, who lacked the experience to oversee the abrasives business, were unable to fill the void. . . .

July 19, 1983, *The Wall Street Journal*
"Bitter Harvest"; "Expanding Too Fast, A Major Grain Co-op Fell Into Big Trouble"; "Agri-Industries is Suffering from Poor Acquisitions, Heavy Losses, U.S. Probe."

July 25, 1983, *Business Week*
"Greyhound: A Big Sell-Off Leaves It Built for Better Speed"
"After years of trying to produce a good return at the meat-processing and packing subsidiary—bought in a 1970 diversification—the Phoenix-based conglomerate admitted defeat on June 29."

August 1, 1983, *Business Week*
"Profit Pains at the New Aetna"
"Diversification has failed to offset losses in underwriting."
"With the exception of real estate development, Aetna's recent forays into non-insurance businesses have failed to produce the cushion against insurance losses that Filer has so long sought."
"Says one investment banker, 'They're obviously way over their heads . . . they can't manage the industries they are in. . . .

August 22, 1983, *Business Week*
"Gerber: Concentrating on Babies Again"
"Attempts to market adult foods failed, and ventures into mail-order life insurance and day-care centers were only modest successes." [Its] "one major diversification acquisition, CW Transport, Inc., an $85 million hauler acquired in 1979, lost $976,000 last year."

August 24, 1983, *The Wall Street Journal*
"Scott Paper Plans to Shed Some Operations"

"Scott Paper Co. said it plans to sell timberlands, furniture, and foam operations, valued at as much as $500 million, as part of a broad push to simplify its business and improve long-term profitability."

August 29, 1983, *Business Week*
"Fuqua: Radical Surgery for a 'Ragtag' Conglomerate"
". . . sold units accounting for two thirds of sales. But while the divestitures slashed sales to $607 million in 1982, Fuqua's net earnings from continuing operations have quadrupled since 1978 to $16.7 million last year. And this year, net income has jumped a titanic 321 percent. . ."

September 12, 1983, *Forbes*
"For years Land O'Lakes was a well-run cooperative. Then it caught expansionitus."

October 10, 1983, *Business Week*
"Why Coca-Cola and Wine Didn't Mix"
"By selling out . . . Coke tacitly cried 'uncle' to Ernest & Julio Gallo . . ."
"Coke set unrealistic goals and did not fully understand the complexities of the wine market."

November 8, 1983, *Business Week*
"Itek: Shedding its eyeglass divison and focusing on high-tech lines"
"There was a sigh of relief at Itek Corp. late last year when the company finally managed to unload its eyeglass-manufacturing business. Shorn of this money-losing division . . ."

its advantage in research, marketing, and manufacturing. Following the leader locks a company into mediocre performance or worse.

Often, it is the case of the blind leading the blind. GM owned Frigidaire, so Ford went out and bought Philco. ITT owned Avis, so RCA acquired Hertz. The fact that neither Frigidaire nor Avis did well for its owners seemed beside the point. The leader must know what it is doing. (Subsequently, GM sold Frigidaire and ITT divested Avis.)

Emulating companies that operate in different fields makes even less sense. Each industry and, in fact, each market segment has its own set of requirements for being a winner. Doing what succeeds in another market, or in industry in general, is no guarantee of success. Each company must develop its own unique array of capabilities that apply to its specific activities.

A need for personal security often lies behind executives' propensity to emulate others. They feel that they are less subject to criticism if they follow policies and practices that have proven successful elsewhere. They become like the money management fraternity and move with the crowd. Woe unto him who acts independently and fails. If he is doing the same as all the others, who can blame him if things turn out badly? One consulting firm has found plenty of clients willing to pay for data correlating return on investment with various characteristics of other companies in other industries. Never mind that what works elsewhere may be counterproductive here. If management can demonstrate that its policies have served other companies well, it feels safe.

Opportunism and emulation of others are two patterns of decision-making that characterize myopic managements without a sound strategy. A third is to look to conventional wisdom for guidance. The futility of trying to apply the old saws to specific situations is the subject of Chapter 3.

# 3

# Conventional Wisdom?

Executives with management myopia are flying blind. Without a clear vision of where their best long-term opportunities lie, they are seduced by whatever looks attractive at the moment. Still, they grope for sound strategic policies. They emulate other companies that seem to be doing well. And they hew to the conventional wisdom.

The conventional wisdom includes a group of adages which are widely accepted as sound guides to management such as:

- Growth is essential to business success.
- Diversification reduces risk and adds to earnings stability.
- Being in related businesses produces synergism.
- A full line represents a competitive advantage.
- Vertical integration adds extra earnings and strength.
- Market share is the key to strategic success.
- Emerging industries offer the best business opportunities.
- The best way to find out what to offer is to ask the customers.''

Each of these old saws is a potential pitfall. Each has led many a company to disaster. None is a reliable guide to strategy in all situations.

## GROWTH

The notion that growth is essential to success has become an obsession in the American business community. It causes companies to run amok, to enter any industry which seems to offer a possibility of increased earnings. It has led innumerable corporations to load themselves up with excess baggage, to squander resources on operations in which they have no reasonable possibility of superior performance.

Companies in mature industries such as petroleum, which are no longer growing but generate large amounts of cash, are particularly susceptible to this kind of error. Exxon lost $700 million in its efforts to achieve growth in office automation. ARCO took a $775 million write-down when it decided to abandon its metals businesses. Ashland Oil posted a $270 million charge against earnings when it retreated from its insurance operations and other diversification. Sohio's investment in copper and abrasives went sour. Montgomery Ward, the main asset in Mobil's $1.7 billion acquisition of Marcor, has been a continuing drag on earnings. Previously, the industry had suffered serious reverses in fertilizers and chemicals.

The obsession with growth pervades the business community. Intelligent executives readily accept the premise that growth is necessary, that it justifies investing in unfamiliar industries. The business press echoes the theme—"Gerber Products Co. had long dominated the U.S. baby food market (its 1978 market share was 69 percent), but a declining birth rate *forced* it to seek growth elsewhere." (*Business Week,* August 22, 1983—italics mine) "Pepperidge Farms expanded beyond its traditional base, feeling *it had little choice,* since the market for frozen, sweet, baked goods has been declining." (*Business Week,* June 4, 1984—italics mine.) Like teenage sex, growth has become imperative, regardless of consequences.

Senior executives should realize that efforts to get bigger are not always wise. Most industries are not growing rapidly. The overall economy is expanding at only a few percent per year, despite the rapid growth of electronics, computers, robotics, exercise salons, fast foods, and bioengineering. Most companies can be more successful in the activities they know best. Companies such as Chase Brass and Nucor Corp. have clearly demonstrated that there is a lot of money to be made in mature industries. As Kenneth Andrews says in *The Concept of Corporate Strategy* (Richard D. Irwin, 1980), the McIlhenny strategy (tabasco sauce only) may not be totally obsolete."

The role of business is to create economic value, to earn a high return on the financial, human, and material resources it employs. When it loses sight of this basic fact and prostrates itself at the altar of growth, it makes the kind of blunders reported in the list of news items beginning on page 25, Chapter 2. Growth can be healthy, but it is not right for all companies in all industries. Most of us will have to be content just doing a superior job of what we do best—and profiting from it.

One of the notions promoting the obsession with growth is the idea that the large corporation can trample any small company that gets in its way. There are indeed activities in which economies of scale provide a decisive advantage. But there are many others where the opposite is true, where the giant corporation is at a disadvantage. GE could not compete successfully with smaller companies in semiconductors and plastic molding. GM failed in major appliances. Spending hundreds of millions of dollars in office automation did not enable Exxon to keep up with smaller firms. The key is the matchup between the capabilities of the firm and the needs of the market place. As a corporation grows, it becomes more able to compete in some areas and less able to compete in others.

## DIVERSIFICATION

Don't carry all your eggs in one basket is an adage we have all heard from childhood. The management fraternity has accepted the notion that having entries in more than one industry reduces risk and helps to stabilize earnings and the price of a company's shares. But the supposed benefits are small, and the dangers are great.

The performance of diversified companies has been disappointing. Companies with closely related operations have been shown to be more profitable. The investment community is disillusioned with conglomerates and accords them mediocre price-earnings ratios. When I reviewed the ratings of diversified companies in Value Line, I found that their stock prices were more volatile and that they were considered no safer than nondiversified firms.

The benefits that sound attractive in theory are difficult to attain in real life. For example, extreme cyclicality has characterized the earnings of the airline industry. TWA decided to solve the problem by diversifying. It bought Canteen Corporation, Hilton International, some fast food chains, and a real estate agency franchise operation. What is found was that cyclicality became an even more serious problem. When the economy turned down, it had several operations in trouble instead of just one. To correct the difficulty it had created, it severed the corporate connection between the businesses by spinning off the airline. Bad as the problems were as a cyclical airline, TWA found that those of a conglomerate were worse.

The process of diversifying is fraught with danger. When it diversifies, top management has to learn a new role. In a single-industry company, the senior executives know the business and are best qualified to make the key decisions. In a diversified corporation, top management cannot know the many business situations as well as its unit managers. Its task changes from making the big decisions to selecting and supervising the general managers who make them. The difference, while subtle, is basic. Many executives are unable to make that change when they lead their companies into diversification. In fact, many fail even to see the need to alter the way they operate.

Getting into a new field is risky, whether a company relies on internal development or on acquisitions. Each new business requires a different approach. One is always inclined to use what he has learned in one industry when he enters another. Often it doesn't work. The experience of untold numbers of companies which have been tripped up by it gives little support to the common view that diversification reduces risk.

## SYNERGISM

Synergism is the process by which each of two things working together enhances the effectiveness of the other, by which "two plus two can equal five." By being in related businesses, a corporation seeks to gain a competitive advantage by sharing technology, marketing, or manufacturing skills among several operating units. Some firms have, in fact, been able to build competitive advantages based on their unique combination of businesses.

But often the pursuit of synergy fails to achieve its goal. The combination of activities must be very carefully chosen. Attempts to coordinate businesses involve substantial costs. Maintaining the expense of the staff to do the coordinating is only one part of the burden. Another is the loss of autonomy and flexibility by the divisions involved. Tied to each other, they can become sluggish and clumsy with key decisions being made by a remote bureaucracy.

The coordination problem is made more difficult by a built-in tendency toward friction between operating units. If they share a resource such as a central research laboratory, manufacturing plant, or sales organization, they squabble about allocation of costs and about getting their fair share of the services provided. If they buy and sell from one another, the bickering gets even worse. Each unit expects preferential treatment from the other. These mutually incompatible expectations often lead to internecine warfare. How far the real world is from the ideal!

When I was at General Electric, it tried another approach to developing synergy. Preserving the autonomy of the operating units, it assigned a number of experienced executives to scour the company looking for opportunities for one division to use the resources of another. Their function was purely advisory; general managers were free to do what they wanted with the suggestions of the staff executives. As far as I could see, nothing was accomplished. The units were already pursuing the resources they needed in their businesses both within and outside of the corporation.

In addition to the practical problems of achieving effective coordination, companies have to cope with the tendency of humans, even senior executives, to build castles in the air. I know. I've been there.

When I become CEO of Ventron Corporation, it manufactured an obscure line of inorganic chemicals called metal hydrides. We soon started another business: supplying rare inorganic chemicals to research laboratories. Later, we entered the chemical specialities business, mixing various compounds for specific industrial uses. For example, we made release agents for the rubber industry and microbiocides to protect plastics from mildew.

From that hodgepodge of grubby little businesses, I concocted a grand scheme. Selling research chemicals would give us insights as to the new directions being taken by the chemical industry and would enable us to identify new synthetic inorganic chemicals to make before others saw the opportunity. Synthesizing chemicals would enable us to make special molecules to serve as bases for new chemical specialties.

This was an idea for going our own way, all right, and for being unique. But it was a pipe dream. Looking back, I wonder that the financial analysts to whom I presented this nonsense were able to keep from laughing. We never achieved synergy. When we finally accepted that four was an acceptable result of two plus two, each of these businesses did quite well.

But the siren song of synergy continues to seduce American businessmen. Because it could sell cigarettes, Philip Morris thought it could sell beer and bought Miller Brewing. It poured millions into an advertising campaign which pushed Miller into the number two position among brewers. It became the synergistic success story of the decade! But eventually Miller's sales growth bogged down, despite the heavy promotional expenditures. Looking back, it appears that Philip Morris never earned a decent return on its venture into beer. Vintners trembled when master marketer Coca-Cola sought to develop synergy by barging into the wine business. But it turned out that the capabilities that made Coke such an outstanding success in soft drinks did not fit the wine industry. Eventually, Coca-Cola withdrew, leaving Gallo more firmly entrenched than ever at the top of the wine business. In each of these cases, two plus two ended up as three.

Synergy is an intriguing concept. But it is a dangerous one as well.

## A FULL LINE

Salesmen can always identify prospects for products and services beyond the scope of what they have to sell. Especially in light of the short-term effects of incremental volume, their recommendations to broaden the line are seductive. But the notion of offering a full line leads away from defining the specific things a firm can do best. Sears Roebuck has had an opportunity to learn that lesson the hard way on more than one occasion. Among the lines it has had to abandon are prebuilt houses, automobiles, mink coats, and oil paintings.

The idea that a full line is necessary has been used to justify a great deal of nonsense. Actually a really full line almost never makes sense. General Motors could hardly afford to manufacture a Jeep, much less a Rolls Royce or a custom-designed limousine. Offering cheap plastic sandals would be insane for a Fifth Avenue boutique specializing in $500 shoes for the elite. The experience of Chase Brass and Nucor Corp. give the lie to the theory that a full line represents a competitive advantage.

Carrying a full line used to be a cornerstone of the strategy of Aerovox Corporation, a manufacturer of capacitors. But its performance was poor. The directors decided that its ceramic capacitor line represented its best opportunity. They split that off as a separate company and sold the other operations to an investor group headed by an ex-employee.

The ceramic capacitor operation did very well. As AVX Corporation, it is a leader in its field. Its stock became worth more than 10 times what it had been when it represented a full-line company. The performance of the business that was sold was also very good. In its last year as part of Aerovox, it lost $1 million on sales of $8 million. Twelve years later as an independent enterprise, it earned over $6 million (pretax) on sales of $56 million.

The management of the old Aerovox was proud of its status as a full-line producer. But when the operations were split up, the results were far better for each separate part. The value of each component is now far more than the combination with a full line was ever worth.

Some companies do in fact cater to customers who demand a wide choice. But they must reckon with the greater cost of manufacturing shorter runs, carrying a heavy inventory, and additional sales training. A decision to carry an unusually broad line is usually tantamount to abandoning the bargain hunter to the low-margin, high-volume supplier. Rather than being a competitive advantage, carrying a full line often renders companies more vulnerable to specialized competition.

## VERTICAL INTEGRATION

"Control your sources of supply" and "get closer to the end user" are precepts that have led many companies to integrate vertically. But what they often find is that a captive outlet serves the customer less well than one that can freely select its sources. Moreover, a vertically integrated firm has less flexibility to adjust to economic changes. For example, users of metal parts have set up their own die-casting plants only to find themselves at a competitive disadvantage when more cost-effective plastic parts became available.

Vertically integrated companies also have to deal with the tendency of sister divisions to squabble. When bonuses and promotions depend on profit performance, transfer pricing, for example, can become a serious bone of contention.

The conventional wisdom holds that a vertically integrated corporation has a competitive advantage. It is thought to be in a better position to cut prices because it earns a profit at several stages of the process. What this notion overlooks is that each step requires its own investment. Setting up a captive source of supply requires capital. If a corporation is less efficient in that operation than independent vendors, the captive operation will not produce an attractive return. This turns into a competitive handicap and makes it *more* difficult to reduce prices and still show an adequate profit. Specialized independent suppliers, subject to the competitive discipline of the market place, are often much more effective than captive operations.

One of the factors contributing to the resurgence of Chrysler Corporation is the fact that it is *less* integrated vertically than its competitors. Chrysler buys about 70 percent of its parts from suppliers versus 50 percent for Ford and 30 percent for GM. Since labor costs the auto makers twice as much as it costs the parts suppliers, Chrysler has a decided competitive advantage. Moreover, it has a wider choice of new technologies. And the suppliers, not Chrysler, have to finance the fixed assets involved.

## MARKET SHARE

The notion that market share is the primary determinant of profitability was given great currency by the Boston Consulting Group and its *growth share matrix*. The work of the Strategic Planning Institute showing a strong correlation between market share and profitability lent further credence to the idea.

The rationale for the strategic importance of market share lies in the notion that the accumulation of experience leads to increased competence. Each time a company's total accumulated experience in producing a product doubled, the theory went, its total cost should decline by 20–30 percent. Thus the market leader, which was accumulating experience fastest, should be the low-cost producer. It should be in a position where it could, if it chose, drive all its competitors from the market. As a result of the spectacular success of BCG, these theories quickly became a part of the conventional wisdom of the business community.

Unfortunately, however, things turn out not to be so simple. In many industries, the largest entrant is not the most profitable. Many small companies, even in "doggy" industries, do quite well. And when the leader is most profitable, it isn't apparent whether leadership led to profitability, profitability led to leadership, or good management led to both.

Actually the whole concept of market share is a slippery one. It depends entirely on how one defines a market. Every customer is different from every other, and how one groups them is a matter of convenience, completely arbitrary. One can say that Nucor makes a higher profit than U.S. Steel in the same market or that Nucor is in a different market entirely.

The emphasis on the importance of market share suggests a policy of sacrificing current profitability to win market leadership.

After seizing the biggest share of the business, a company expects to cash in by having the lowest costs in the industry. But such a strategy can lead to disaster. Where several firms follow the same course, all can lose, as happened in the home computer industry. In other cases, the market is slow to respond to lower prices, and leadership may not be worth its cost.

The ultimate goal in any case is to develop the capability to serve customers more effectively than competitors. Focusing on building market share approaches this objective indirectly, buying market share at some cost assuming that superior capability will develop as a result. But one can get better results by focusing directly on identifying the specific capabilities needed for success and working to build them.

## EMERGING INDUSTRIES

Spectacular success stories associated with emerging industries stir one's imagination. Companies spend enormous amounts of energy and money trying to enter the next explosive growth area. But emerging industries are easy to recognize. They attract too many competitors and too much capital. The average return on investment is often lower there than in more stable environments.

For example, when it became apparent that semiconductors were headed for explosive growth, a dozen companies invested in facilities for making the primary raw material, silicon wafers. Almost all, including competent firms such as Du Pont, Merck, and W. R. Grace, lost money and were forced to withdraw. The same thing has begun in personal computers and software, in robots, and in genetic engineering. Even when the leaders in floppy discs began losing money because of overcapacity, still more companies, including Dennison and Eastman Kodak, plunged in.

Videotapes are another emerging industry. Unit sales nearly quadrupled between 1982 and 1984. But with more than 60 companies competing for that business, the average wholesale price dropped from $11.34 to $6.58 and was expected to continue falling in 1985. A wholesale shakeout seemed inevitable. Few producers, if any, would ever see a decent return on their investment.

As in more prosaic fields, the only winners in emerging industries are companies with superior capabilities to serve specific market segments. But because projections of rapid growth lure so many to enter these businesses, even the most capable firms frequently fail to achieve attractive results.

## ASK THE CUSTOMERS

The management fraternity is well aware of the dangers of offering a new product that no one will buy such as the Edsel. The problem is not knowing what the customer wants. The solution, says the conventional wisdom, is to ask customers what they need, to do the market research required to determine what people will buy.

There is danger in offering only products that customers say they will buy. All of the suppliers are asking the same questions and getting the same answers. They develop similar products and are back on the old treadmill.

Determining what customers will buy is not so simple as just asking them. Often they do not know or will not say. The outstanding business successes usually result from suppliers seeing needs which the customers themselves may not recognize. It requires vision and courage to lead, to pioneer.

When the technology to produce dry copiers was first developed, the market for them did not exist. Asking companies how many they would buy was futile. As a result of accepting the approach of supplying only recognized market needs, company after company turned its back on the technology. Finally, little Haloid Corporation saw the potential, bought the technology, and turned itself into giant Xerox Corporation.

Even after Xerox machines were available, people couldn't grasp the magnitude of the potential market. The company I was working for at the time did a careful study of its needs in order to determine what size Xerox copier to buy. When the machine was installed, its usage level was *seven times* what the study had forecast!

Ventron Corporation developed a superior chemical for protecting vinyl plastics against mildew. Sales grew rapidly. When they reached the $1 million level, Ventron hired a market research firm to determine how large the potential market was. They had a young man ask the customers how many prospective uses they had for the product where it was not yet being used. Based on the answers, he concluded that Ventron had saturated the market and should stop wasting money in a futile attempt to build sales.

What actually happened was that volume kept right on growing. Customer personnel simply had not been willing to admit that they had failed to incorporate Ventron's mildew proofing in products that really needed it. The market researcher lacked the vision to see the need and the opportunity.

Knowledge of the market and what customers will and will not buy can be one of a company's most valuable resources. But what is needed is more than blindly following what the customer *says* he wants. A supplier needs vision and insight of his own to identify the opportunities that can lead to outstanding results.

## CONVENTIONAL WISDOM OR A GAME PLAN?

For those suffering from management myopia, the conventional wisdom is a welcome palliative. It provides an acceptable basis for an elaborate stategy statement to be used with both company executives and outsiders such as financial analysts. "This company's objective is to grow at least 10 percent annually. It aims to reduce risk and to increase earnings stability through carefully planned diversification. It will develop synergism between its operations to achieve competitive advantages. It will enhance its leadership position by offering a full line. It will exploit opportunities to increase earnings through vertical integration. It will maintain or achieve leadership positions in each market it enters. At the same time, it will pursue opportunities to use its strengths (technical/manufacturing/marketing) to enter emerging markets to take advantage of exciting new growth opportunities."

Who could fault such a statement? Who could fail to appreciate the wisdom and broad perspective of its authors? We have all been taught the value of these precepts. The only question that remains is how effectively we can execute. So we are back to the simple question of who can be motivated to try harder on the competitive treadmill.

Such strategic pap may give top management a warm feeling, but it doesn't produce results. Business success depends not on generalizations but on the specific capabilities an organization brings to bear on each of its markets. A strategy must define which market segments are to be served, identify which capabilities will produce success, and provide a program to develop superiority in those areas.

A game plan must provide a blueprint for winning. A football coach who can offer nothing more than an exhortation to make touchdowns by running and passing and to shut down the opponent's offense is not helping his players know what to do. He must plan who is to run where and when, what passing plays to call and when, so as to take advantage of his team's specific strengths and the opponent's weaknesses.

The heart of a business strategy is the determination of which capabilities to develop to achieve dominance in the targeted market segments. It is in the matchup between the customer's specific requirements and the company's ability to meet them. Conventional wisdom does not contribute to strategy. To the contrary, for many it serves to mask the fact that the company has no strategy at all.

What's *your* game plan? Is it a practical guide to how you will achieve and maintain leadership in your targeted markets? Or is it a meaningless litany of business adages adapted to the terminology of your particular industry? Does it point the way to building your own unique place in the sun? Or does it leave you to try to get ahead by pursuing the opportunity of the moment or by emulating other companies?

# 4

# The Courage to Be Different

The best one can expect from bumbling blindly about, emulating others, and clinging to conventional wisdom is mediocrity. Achieving superior results requires the vision and courage to be different, to define a unique economic role, and to build the special competence needed to fill it well. It requires a top management that will commit itself to leadership.

To lead in business is to find better ways to serve carefully defined customer groups. It does not necessarily require technical sophistication. It does not necessarily mean offering imaginative products. It does not necessarily entail delivering the highest quality. The basis for leadership is matching the needs of defined customer groups with the capabilities to serve them.

IBM did not invent the mainframe computer nor did it pioneer in personal computers. Few would argue that McDonald's are the best hamburgers in the world. Toys "R" Us carries the same items as many department stores. Yet each of these companies is a leader and has achieved outstanding success. They equipped themselves to serve their targeted customers better than any competitor could.

Companies can lead by deliberately avoiding technological innovation. For example, National Vendors has for years been the number one producer of vending machines for food and cigarettes. It has deliberately eschewed radical technological innovation. When competitors would introduce fancy new features, National Vendors would wait to observe customer reaction and product performance. Often the new equipment was plagued by bugs. Only after an innovation had demonstrated customer appeal and National Vendors was confident it would not cause problems in customer locations, would it incorporate the new feature in its line. Its record of delivering reliability and value was more important to the vending machine operators than being first with each new gimmick.

Other companies in other markets have pursued different routes to success. Xerox, 3M, and Polaroid established themselves as major corporations by pioneering new products. K mart based its success on developing outstanding competence in merchandising. Brooks Brothers created a unique aura as a quality clothier. Each of these companies became a leader by going its own way and building a superior capability to serve its particular groups.

Sometimes an executive with the courage to be different develops a successful new approach to management that becomes a pattern for a whole group of followers. Under Royal Little, for example, Textron Corporation became the prototype conglomerate. More recently Bairnco Corporation has pioneered a new concept of diversification. For years, it had been a highly successful conventional diversified corporation. Now, its objective "is to grow a family of separate companies with single, or focused, product lines" that "may become independent public companies through distribution of shares to Bairnco stockholders." The first such spin-off, Kaydon Corporation, became an independent enterprise in 1984. It will be interesting to follow Bairnco's progress and to see whether this becomes a new type of corporate activity.

Having the courage to be different is not enough. A leader also needs vision. It is the courageous executive with management myopia who runs amok, who reaches for any opportunity in sight. He is a loose cannon. If he is lucky, he may stumble into great good fortune for a time. But in the long run he will devote too much energy and capital to businesses in which the odds are too long against him. Ultimately, a successor will have to clean up the mess he has created. If the courageous executive is to succeed over the long pull, he must see clearly where he is heading.

## OVERCOMING MANAGEMENT MYOPIA

To conquer management myopia is to acquire vision. Business vision includes two things. One is the ability to see the basic economic factors that determine which company prospers and which fails. The second is the ability to identify the reasonably possible future developments and to evaluate their potential impact on the business situation. Vision enables an executive to see where to allocate his effort and his capital in order to produce the most favorable results.

---

**WAYS TO OVERCOME MANAGEMENT MYOPIA**
1. Pursue a varied career path.
2. Participate in outside management activities.
3. Learn from others.
4. Use computer games and simulation.
5. Continue to study.
6. Think in concrete terms.
7. Focus on return on capital.

---

People are not born with vision. It is an acquired skill. A manager can learn the factors that affect earnings. He can learn to identify most of the possibilities with which he may have to deal in the future. He can overcome management myopia by applying himself to that task.

The first and most fundamental requirement for developing vision is to realize that it is possible and that it is important. If an executive believes that all that matters is effort, operational expertise, and opportunism, he is unlikely to perceive the pervasive influence of more basic factors on results. If he believes that the future is completely unpredictable or that the best one can do is to base his actions on a single, most likely scenario, he is unlikely to see where the best opportunities and most serious risks are hidden. To see, one must look.

If you want to acquire broad business vision, you have a wide range of approaches available to you. We shall briefly discuss those listed in the box above.

### Pursue a Varied Career Path

Years of unrelenting pressure on line executives to produce short-term results can cause management myopia. That kind of experience can be debilitating with respect to developing the broad vision needed in top management. One cannot help but notice the number of captains of industry who reached their positions without the usual 20–30 years of clawing one's way up through the ranks.

Alfred Sloan, for example, entered top management at Hyatt Roller Bearing only a few years out of MIT thanks to an investment by his father. When he founded Apple Computer, Steven Jobs had had very little exposure to the pressures that cause management myopia. A high proportion of the movers and shakers of our economy started in a family business, in finance, in a profession, or as an entrepreneur. Their backgrounds encouraged looking at business broadly and objectively so as to see the big picture.

Obviously, not all of us have the opportunity to start our careers from the perspective of an owner. But the American business tradition provides the opportunity to develop a rich and varied business background. One can shift back and forth between operating companies and service firms such as consulting companies, auditors, banks, law firms, trade associations, and business publications. Harold Geneen, for example, worked for a time as a consultant. Other top corporate executives have gained a different perspective on business from positions in government.

Within a single company, alternating between line and staff assignments can help minimize management myopia. In the line, one learns how to lead people, to make things happen economically and on time. In staff work, he learns to analyze, to recommend, to persuade others. This combination of experiences can enhance the vision of a receptive mind. One of the strengths of Japanese companies is their practice of systematically rotating managers from one department to another. Their executives develop a broader understanding of their companies and of the factors affecting their corporations' success or failure.

## Participate in Outside Management Activities

Regardless of one's position in his company, he has opportunities to develop vision by assuming responsibility in other organizations. Even as children, we participate in entrepreneurial activities such as selling lemonade, magazines, or newspapers. The president of a steel company told me that one of his most broadening experiences was running the laundry in his university at a profit. As adults, we can broaden our viewpoint by actively managing whatever financial assets we have been able to accumulate.

Executives have unlimited opportunities to gain management experience in nonprofit organizations such as hospitals, churches, museums, charities, social service groups, fraternal organizations, and other civic and cultural organizations. Accepting responsibility in an industry association affords a fine opportunity to look more objectively at one's own business while becoming acquainted with one's peers in other companies. Volunteer executives as well as young people can learn from the entrepreneurial experience of Junior

Achievement. Government bodies such as school boards, water districts, and town councils need management talent. Looking objectively at management problems elsewhere helps one be more objective about his own.

A few years after I became CEO of Ventron Corporation, I was invited to join the board of another small firm. After checking with my directors, I accepted the invitation. It turned out to be a highly rewarding experience.

What I soon learned was that as an outside director, I looked at this new enterprise quite differently from how I viewed my own. Knowing little of the details of the business, I was forced to deal with broader and more basic issues. I could be more objective. I was able to see things the CEO of this other firm had missed. I soon found myself looking at my own company with a fresh, and perhaps more humble, perspective.

Based on that experience, I accepted opportunities to serve on other boards as time would permit. I found that these experiences enhanced my performance as a CEO more than anything else I did in the way of self-development. As I learned to see the problems and opportunities in these other companies, I developed more ability to see my own.

Opportunities to serve on the boards of small companies are open to more than CEOs. These companies need help. Providing it can be an extremely rewarding and broadening experience.

## Learn from Others

In most companies, there seem to be a few managers who have somehow avoided management myopia and see more clearly than others. Identifying these people, talking to them, seeing how they think, and listening to their ideas can help other executives develop their own ability to see.

Top management has an excellent opportunity to broaden its vision through its contacts with the company's independent directors. As experienced, objective outsiders with a serious responsibility for the company's well-being, they bring a different perspective to management. Unfortunately, many managements seem to feel it necessary to spend the bulk of their time talking to the directors— trying to inform or to persuade them. The function of the board is not limited to absorbing information but includes advising and supporting management. Top executives would benefit by doing more listening and less talking in board meetings.

As a young president, I insisted on several occasions that the directors approve proposals to which they were obviously cool. With the passage of time, I observed a correlation between the views of the board and the results we achieved. Some of the projects I had bulled through came to an unfortunate end. Eventually, I learned to listen more carefully, to seek out ideas from directors, and to take better advantage of one of the company's significant assets.

In other circumstances, such as in social settings or in the political arena, one is exposed to different thought patterns and ways of approaching problems. Some are superficial or obviously biased. Others reflect wisdom and insight. By listening carefully one can add to his arsenal of approaches to meeting problems.

One can also learn indirectly from others by following the business press. As one reads about successes and failures and ponders their causes, he looks beyond the rough-and-tumble of his daily routine and sees more basic relationships. When he reads news items like the ones on pages 25 and 26, Chapter 2, he begins to question why so many companies go wrong. He knows that these blunders were made by intelligent executives trying to build their companies. As he sees the ravages of management myopia, he can see the importance of gaining a broader, more objective view of the issues in his own situation.

## Use Computer Games and Simulation

Business games played on a computer are useful devices for broadening vision. Typically one or a group of executives manages a company in competition with others. Each has an opportunity to set prices and to allocate spending to advertising, selling, R&D, cost reduction, manufacturing capacity, inventories, or other factors. After each round of decisions, the inputs of the participants are fed into the computer which then produces reports as to how each competitor has fared. The process is repeated a number of times. Each participant tries to determine the key determinants of success and how best to allocate his resources.

For perceptive executives, these games can impart vision. Operating skills play no part in the game. Participants' attention is focused on strategic factors such as capital allocation, marketing mix, and competitive position. Such games force executives with the opportunity to deal with the kind of basic economic factors often obscured by the demands of day-to-day problems in real life.

Managers can try various strategies without the risks of actual losses.

Computer simulation of a company's own situation also provides executives with an opportunity to focus on fundamental relationships and to see the company in broader perspective. They observe the projected results of alternative courses of action under different assumptions. Many senior executives are enthusiastic about the way that computer simulation is helping them gain more insight as to the key factors affecting their long-term results.

## Continue to Study

Today, executives have a wealth of opportunities to participate in continuing education. Thousands of courses, workshops, and seminars are available on almost every conceivable topic. Discussions with other executives enrolled in these educational programs can lead to new ways of approaching a problem. Scores of books on business appear every year.

Exposure to new ideas and new ways of thinking provides opportunities to add to one's vision. But if one seeks only technical skills from these activities, that will be all he gets.

A subject that is especially important to businessmen and that often gets short shrift is microeconomics—the economics of the firm. A grasp of economic principles can be extremely helpful in evaluating strategic choices. A thorough grounding in economics can contribute to sound business judgment. It is also conducive to the following two ways of thinking that help broaden vision.

## Think in Concrete Terms

The ability of the human mind to make abstractions sets our species apart from the others. It provides us with enormous power to solve problems. But unless we systematically test our abstractions against concrete reality, they may lead us astray.

For example, executives are sometimes entranced with the notion of defining their business with a simple abstract notion. Being an energy company sounds like a fine strategic concept. But how does skill in discovering and producing fluid hydrocarbons help to sell gasoline or home heating oil, to say nothing of producing electricity from atomic power or finding ways to reduce fuel consumption in an office building? Offering a full line of financial services sounds like a dandy idea. But how do the specific capabilities of an insurance company, a bank, or a credit card operation add to the profitability of a stock brokerage in practical day-to-day operating terms? Managing a portfolio of operations so that the positive cash flows of the mature businesses exactly match the needs of the growing units sounds like a sophisticated strategic approach. But where and how much does that add to the productivity of the units? And what are the costs?

A sound game plan requires going beyond glib generalizations and superficial appearances. For a strategic move to be economically effective, it must contribute to productivity, to providing better value to customers. The practice of thinking about the real, tangible implications of a move helps one see it more clearly. For example, integrating the sales forces of Company A and Company B which sell to the same customers sounds great. But how much time will be saved by having one salesman talk about both lines? What is the effect on the salesmen's product knowledge when he must handle the two lines? In customer organizations, do Companies A and B deal with the same people?

Habitually trying to visualize the concrete, nuts-and-bolts results of potential actions can help one see more clearly what kind of game plan is likely to lead to success.

## Focus on Return on Capital

Our obsession with growth and our preoccupation with current earnings divert attention from our more basic task of producing a return on investment. That obligation runs not only to the investor but to society as a whole. The business community is responsible for doing as much as can be done with the resources available to it. The relationship between value created and the resources used is fundamental.

When we lose sight of the capital required to generate sales and earnings, we blunder. We misallocate capital. We squander resources. We divert assets from where they could do the most good and channel them into inferior uses.

Marketing and distribution companies often begin producing what they are selling "in order to get the manufacturing profit, too." They often overlook what they must invest to get it. When the return on investment in production is less than in marketing, such a move is a drag on overall corporate performance. Such companies would usually do better to invest more in the marketing operations, where their skills lie and which provides a higher return.

In the long run, our return on capital affects our ability to grow or even to survive. It affects the cash available to plow back into the business. It affects the willingness of investors to put money into the company. It is a basic determinant of business success.

## VISION AND CHARACTER

Overcoming management myopia and developing vision help executives to see their long-term opportunities and dangers and to set a wise course for the future. The progress the company makes also depends on its character, meaning qualities such as courage, integrity, and tough-mindedness. Corporate character affects not only a company's choice of objectives but its willingness to make the hard decisions necessary to achieve them.

The character of an enterprise reflects the character of the chief executive. If he has broad vision, a strong sense of commitment, and self-discipline, he is likely to impart these qualities to the organization. A critical task of leadership is to develop an organizational character that will foster the setting and achieving of ambitious goals.

Vision affects character. When one sees clearly what one can accomplish in the long term, he finds it easier to make the short-term sacrifices that may be needed. But an executive who cannot see where he is headed vacillates and pursues whatever opportunity comes into view. It is by helping an organization see what it can achieve over time that a leader leads best.

Character affects vision. It requires courage to face dangers; it is easier to ignore them and to hope they will go away. A tendency toward wishful thinking can interfere with the ability to see a situation clearly. An executive or an organization that does not flinch from looking squarely at serious problems is much more likely to see what must be done and to do it. By leading the way in facing problems without fear, a chief executive builds the ability of his lieutenants to do the same.

Vision and character help determine a company's objectives. An enlightened management will realize that the primary function of business activity is to create economic value, to bring together labor, materials, and capital to produce goods and services people will buy. It will seek to profit through activities congruent with the public interest.

Those with less vision and character tend to focus more narrowly on current profits however they can be made. They seek to warp the system to their advantage regardless of the cost to others. They engage in what Harvard's Robert Reich calls *paper entrepreneurialism,* the manipulation of the symbols of wealth rather than in the creation of genuine economic value. They seek to profit from acquisition arithmetic, schemes to avoid taxes, greenmail, and other ploys lacking in intrinsic economic value.

Some executives and some companies succeed in enriching themselves through such machinations. But a strategy based on such approaches is vulnerable. Living by the law of the jungle is a dangerous game. Other predators abound. People, through their government, continue to modify the rules of the game to reduce opportunities to profit without delivering economic value. Skills developed to exploit anomalies in the system become worthless when the anomalies are eliminated. Companies are on firmer ground when they pursue profits through creating real value.

Even a company dedicated to serving its customers well has difficulty in determining which courses of action will be best. In particular, it must decide how much emphasis to put on activities generating current earnings and how much to put on developing the capabilities needed to prosper later on. Financial performance criteria such as return on sales or on equity do not reflect the potential value of investments in capabilities to serve customers more effectively in the future. Some corporations that appear to be doing well are robbing from tomorrow to feed today. Others with more modest current results are creating great value in terms of future prospects.

One of the strengths of Japanese industry lies in the objectives it pursues. Japanese companies are oriented to the long run. Their first priority is the well-being of their permanent employees. Growth, profits, innovation, and prestige are seen as elements in a program to serve the long-term interests of the corporate family. With this orientation, Japanese executives are better equipped to deal wisely with the trade-offs between immediate earnings and future competitive strength. They are often prepared to spend years of profitless effort when they see that it will lead to the kind of leadership position so many Japanese companies now enjoy.

Achieving a matchup between capabilities and market needs is a sound strategy for countries as well as for companies. Individualism is a more pronounced cultural trait of the United States than of many other countries, and especially of Japan. Having the courage to be different is a potential competitive advantage for American executives and companies and for the economy as a whole.

# 5

# Whose Game Plan?

Who is in the best position to determine which strategy to follow? In professional football and basketball, the head coach decides on the game plan. The players only carry it out. But in business, the CEO is responsible for both strategy and execution. When he has management myopia and confines his company to a competitive treadmill or runs amok, everyone suffers the consequences.

Athletic clubs have good reason to assign responsibility for the game plan to the coach rather than to the players. The coach has more experience. The players have enough challenge in developing the skills and physical and mental conditioning to be fully effective in action. In the midst of the contest, players often lack the objectivity needed to identify and to pursue the best plan of attack. The coach and his staff have a better opportunity to see the team in broad perspective and to determine the approach most likely to win.

Rather than a coach and his staff, a corporation has a board of directors. It is in a better position to see a business situation in broad context than the CEO. It has more experience. It should be more objective. Its views are less likely to be distorted by personal interests or by relationships within the organization. It is less preoccupied by operating problems. It represents a potentially valuable source of assistance to the CEO in determining what game plan to follow.

Few companies make full use of their boards in formulating strategy. Many CEOs feel that active board participation in this function would encroach upon their authority and weaken their position. They prefer to choose their own direction rather than to implement plans formulated by others. Some fail to see how independent directors with limited knowledge of the company and its industry could provide sound counsel. Their objective is to get board approval of their own strategies as painlessly as possible.

Actually, a board of directors has two roles to play with respect to a company's game plan. One is to advise and assist top management in formulating strategy. This is not a formal board responsibility but is still an activity in which it can make an important contribution to corporate success. The second role is in the fiduciary responsibility to see that the company is well managed. If management fails to pursue a sound strategy, the board has an obligation to take action to correct the problem.

Some CEOs are excellent strategists. Even these can benefit from soliciting the views of independent directors who may see the company more objectively or may have specialized experience relative to the situation. But a board can feel comfortable delegating responsibility for strategy formulation to such an executive, just as some coaches give the quarterback wide latitude in play selection.

Other chief executives, who may be outstanding in their ability to get things done, are less effective in formulating strategy. Such managers, if they are wise, will enlist the active help of their boards in developing their game plans. If they do not, responsible directors will initiate action to improve their companies' strategies. In all too many cases, however, neither the CEO nor the board acts to secure the participation of directors in the strategy formulation process. Failure to exploit this potentially valuable resource has led many a company to disaster.

## THE BOARD AS ADVISORS

Each of us, even the most gifted chief executive, has his weaknesses. Each of us has biases and blind spots. Each of us is more competent in some areas than in others. Each of us has had only so much experience to guide his decisions and actions. Each of us, relying only on his own vision and insights, will occasionally fail to see important opportunities or dangers. Each of us will make mistakes.

We have already considered the powerful factors that cause management myopia. Overcoming it is a relative thing, not absolute. The vision of even the most clear-sighted executive is still warped to some extent by his situation, his experience, his associates, and his personal interests. Each of these factors contributes to the chances that a chief executive, acting solely on his own counsel, will blunder.

Independent directors are in a better position to see a company's situation in broad perspective. Collectively, their experience covers a far greater range. Often a board will include members with expertise in certain functional areas such as finance, marketing, manufacturing, or personnel exceeding that of any of the company's managers. Directors' fields of vision are not distorted by close relationships with nor obligations to other members of management. They are not dependent on the company for their livelihood. They can be much more objective in considering alternative strategies for the company and for its component parts.

Whether a chief executive avails himself of the experience, objectivity, and wisdom of the board in devising a game plan for his company depends on two things. The first is whether he has the vision to see the need for sound strategy and understands what it is. The second is whether he feels sufficiently secure in his own position to risk exposing his blind spots by drawing on the insights and judgment of others. If he is determined to play God and maintain complete freedom to pursue his own inclinations, he will want little board participation in strategy formulation. In fact, he will resist any attempt by the board to induce him to commit even his own strategy to writing because it could limit his freedom of action.

This is often apparent when a board asks a CEO bent on acquisitions to state the criteria he intends to use in the selection process. Realizing that acquisition prospects are hard to find, many CEOs avoid preparing guidelines with sufficient specificity to exclude any possibility. They do not want to create for themselves the potential problem of having to justify buying a business that falls outside the parameters they have established.

A chief executive who invites board participation in formulating strategy usually finds the experience rewarding. At least some of his directors will have insights and suggestions that can be valuable to him and to the company. Moreover, when a board has genuinely participated in developing a game plan, the CEO can count on the more enthusiastic support of the directors as he tries to implement it, whether or not he encounters difficulties. When a CEO asks the board for no more than a rubber stamp of a strategy he has prepared, he can expect carping from his directors if things don't go well later on.

## THE BOARD AS THE GOVERNING BODY

The board of directors has overall authority over and responsibility for a corporation. It is at the very top of the organization chart. It selects the chairman, president, and other officers, which it can also remove. Theoretically, at least, it is the institutional mechanism through which the owners exercise control over what they own.

The responsibilities of the directors extend beyond the financial interests of the shareholders. They also have an obligation to consider the interests of the company's other constituencies such as the employees, the customers, the communities in which it operates, and the general public. The directors are the individuals to whom not only the owners, but society as a whole entrusts the assets of the corporation and their use. How well they perform their duties affects not only their stockholders' wealth but the economic well-being of us all.

The board of directors is not expected to manage the business but to govern it. Its job is to provide for effective management, not to perform it. It selects the top executives and oversees their activities. If the persons it selects do not perform properly, it is responsible for taking action to correct the problem. An effective board will advise management and do what it can to help the CEO to get better results. If this fails, the board must act to get better management.

The board must assure itself that management is acting not only to generate attractive current results but also to provide for the future. Management must safeguard the value of the company's assets, tangible and intangible. It must develop the resources and capabilities needed to exploit the opportunities available to it. The board must determine whether management is in fact meeting these responsibilities.

A corporation's strategy has a pervasive influence on the results it achieves. A board must satisfy itself that management has formulated and is pursuing a sound, coherent strategy. If it is not, the board is responsible for seeing that management takes corrective action. The alternative is often simply to wait until a myopic CEO gets himself into such serious trouble that he has to be removed.

Similarly, the board of directors must see to it that a company prepares adequate plans, not only for operations but also for developing the resources it will need in the future. In the area of planning there is less a board can do itself; it must require operating management to perform the job. A responsible board cannot tolerate a failure to prepare plans that consider the range of reasonably possible developments and the responses available to the company.

The board of directors must provide for sound corporate policies. In a few areas such as dividend policy the responsibility of the board is widely recognized. There it plays an active role in policymaking. Social responsibility is another area in which some boards take the initiative in policy formulation. But in all phases of the business, whether management or the board takes the laboring oar, the board is responsible for seeing that appropriate policies are established and followed.

The general character and culture of a corporation affects its performance. Often, it is difficult for operating management to perceive how its patterns of behavior compare with those in other companies. Independent directors are in a better position to see when a company has too much dead wood or is understaffed, is overly bureaucratic or is too ready to shoot from the hip, lacks discipline or is too miserly about investing in the future, is too willing or too reluctant to delegate responsibility, is too idealistic or too ready to compromise ethical values. The board is responsible for seeing that the company develops a culture and a character that will serve the interests of both its owners and other interested parties.

Finally, the directors are responsible for their own performance. If the board is to be effective, it must recognize its responsibilities and meet them. This is the most difficult challenge of them all. Directors are subject to the same kind of myopia about their own performance as operating managers are about theirs.

## THE DIRECTOR'S DILEMMA

What directors actually do is determined by more than the relevant statutes governing corporations. It is affected by what management and others expect of the board. It is influenced by an informal set of "rules of the game" described by Professor Thomas Whisler in his book by that name (Dow Jones-Irwin, 1984). Rule I(B) commands, "Support your CEO." Rule II(C) is "We don't manage the company." Rule II(D) says specifically, "We don't set strategy." Rule VII(A), concerning removing the CEO, cautions, "Don't rush." Except in a crisis, directors tend to go along with the CEO.

An independent director who wants to do his job and is concerned about the direction his company is taking is in a difficult position. His colleagues expect him to abide by the rules of the game and discourage dissension. Moreover, his relationship with the CEO tends to be an awkward one.

An important part of any manager's job is to help his employees do a better job. A basic responsibility of the board of directors is to assist the CEO. But there are important differences in the relationship between the board and the CEO as compared to that between an executive and his subordinates.

Perhaps most important of these differences lies in the nature of the CEO's role. He is the company's leader, the father figure to the employees, the chief spokesman to the outside world. The company's strategies, policies, and plans must be *his* strategies, policies, and plans if he is to lead. It should not be surprising, then, to find directors with the attitude: "When I go to a board meeting, I ask myself only one basic question—'Do we have the right CEO?' If the answer is yes, there is nothing more for me to do. If the answer is no, we must get a new one. That's all there is to being a director."

But things are not so simple as that. As we commented earlier, we all have blind spots and areas of relative weakness. A good board will recognize the weaknesses of the CEO and help him find ways to offset them.

Moreover, the interests of the CEO and those of the company are rarely identical. What will produce the greatest financial reward for the chief executive may not yield the best results for the shareholders. Or what is best for both may be inconsistent with any generally acceptable view of a company's responsibility to its employees or to its community. We have seen executives yield to greenmailers to protect their jobs. We have seen them grant themselves extravagant "golden parachutes." The game plans CEOs pursue are to some extent, at least, influenced by their own personal interests at the expense of those of the shareholders.

The divergence of interests goes far beyond money alone. Being a CEO offers many other potential rewards. The head of a corporation is endowed with the trappings of his office. Some set out to build monuments to themselves, not only in their quarters and perquisites but in the company itself and what it does. Some are obsessed with growth and exhibit acquisition fever. Others seek fame through technical innovation and squander corporate funds on research, the primary purpose of which is glory for the CEO. Still others use their offices to achieve recognition as philanthropists or patrons of the arts by diverting company funds to pet personal projects. Sometimes their game plans are tailored to their own tenure, aimed at achieving personal goals while they are in office.

Make no mistake about it, being head of a corporation can be an exhilarating experience. The rewards in terms of money, recognition, power, and freedom of action can be enormous. The CEO has the opportunity to pursue self-realization in whatever direction seems most attractive to him. His subordinates are in no position to object. To the contrary, they usually find it to their advantage to encourage the boss in his interests, even when they see weaknesses in them. Only the board stands between the CEO and his freedom to abuse his authority.

The natural result is a sort of uneasy accommodation between the CEO and the board. The CEO is overtly respectful, even obsequious, to the board. He provides posh facilities, personal services, even carries directors' brief cases. But an underlying objective in his dealings with directors is to preserve his own freedom of action.

The board is responsible for representing shareholder interests. It must govern, providing for management that will safeguard and build the value of the corporation's assets. To do this, it must support the chief executive it selects. But the CEO's interests are different from those of the owners and other stakeholders. Inevitably, the game plan he selects reflects his own personal interests at some cost to the shareholders. Therein lies the dilemma of the director.

## PRACTICAL CONSIDERATIONS

The ability of the independent director to deal with the situation is narrowly circumscribed. He lives in a real world in which custom and tradition play important parts. He must follow the rules of the game.

In most companies, directors are in fact chosen by the CEO. Even in companies in which prospective new directors are selected by a nominating committee, the CEO's views are solicited before a formal invitation is issued. While it may be difficult, most CEOs are also in a position to get rid of a director who causes problems.

So while in theory the CEO serves at the pleasure of the board, in practice the opposite is closer to the truth.

The power of the CEO is further enhanced by the mechanics of board operations. The CEO generally controls the board meeting agenda. He decides what information is presented to the board and what is withheld. Especially in larger corporations, the CEO often is the chairman of the board and presides at meetings. Commonly, most of the board's time is taken up by administrative detail and by management presentations. Directors have little opportunity to initiate in-depth consideration of basic issues that could prove embarrassing to the CEO.

The board's position is weak, despite its position at the top of the organization. With rare exceptions, the board has no staff and consequently very little independent information-gathering capability. On those occasions when it instructs management to take action, its ability to require compliance is feeble. The following examples are drawn from personal experience as an independent director of several different companies:

- A board was concerned that a company's accounting was overly aggressive in reporting earnings. The chairman of the audit committee of the board put the question to outside auditors who confirmed that the company's accounting practices were far more aggressive than average. The board instructed the CEO to adopt more conservative policies. A year later, the question was repeated, and the auditors responded that there had been no change. The problem continued until a new CEO came upon the scene.
- It appeared to independent directors of another company that it had far too large a corporate staff. It so advised the CEO, but no significant action was taken. The CEO, in better command of the facts, was able to justify every position. Unconvinced, the board continued unsuccessfully to press for a reduction in the corporate office. The situation was not resolved until the board instigated a major reorganization of the company, primarily for other reasons.
- The CEO and major owner of a corporation lived modestly and prided himself on taking a far lower salary than CEOs of other companies of comparable size. His independent directors recognized that his low salary tended to depress the compensation of his subordinates and was making it difficult to

attract adequate management talent. He steadfastly refused to yield to their urging that he increase his own compensation and that of other senior executives.

- Outside directors of a fast-growing, high-technology company recognized a weakness in middle management talent and in administrative procedures and financial control. Repeated recommendations from the board to improve the situation yielded little tangible result. Eventually, the company got into serious financial trouble stemming largely from basic problems that the directors had been calling to the CEO's attention for years.

- The CEO of another high-technology company was committed to building a leading position in Industry A. One of the companies he acquired in that industry happened to have a small operation in Industry B. Almost unnoticed, that little business grew rapidly, earning an outstanding return on investment. The divisions in Industry A languished and performed poorly. Seeing what was happening, outside directors urged the CEO to allocate more resources to Industry B, the company's most attractive area of opportunity. The CEO, however, continued to pour resources into "his baby," Industry A. Ultimately, the operation in Industry B, even with minimum encouragement from the top, became the dominant part of the enterprise. The company's record has been outstanding, almost by accident.

Each of these issues was strategic, involving questions of resource allocation or long-term capabilities. In each case, the board was unwilling to act with sufficient determination to correct the problem. And in each case the company, and often the CEO as well, suffered as a consequence.

## TOWARD MORE EFFECTIVE BOARDS

Success in business requires having a winning game plan. A basic responsibility of a board of directors is to see to it that management formulates a sound strategy and develops effective long-range plans. Too often, directors fail to meet this responsibility and permit their companies to get into trouble.

Some who recognize the need for more effective boards have suggested government action. Directors should be held accountable, they say, and should be more vulnerable to stockholder lawsuits or to fines or other penalties imposed by political authority.

In the 70s, after the well-publicized collapse of Penn Central, it appeared that personal liability of directors might become a serious matter. Directors who grossly neglected their duties and failed even to attend board meetings were found liable for negligence. Because of concern about liability, competent executives became less willing to serve as directors. When faced with important decisions, directors became more likely to choose the course least likely to involve them in lawsuits, rather than what they considered best for the company. The trend toward personal liability for directors turned out to be counterproductive.

Harold Williams, head of the SEC under President Carter, campaigned for more responsible boards. He urged the business community to take action, arguing that if it did not, governmental interference was inevitable.

Williams recommended more independence and authority for the board. He proposed that the office of the chairman of the board be kept separate from that of the CEO. He favored the selection of new directors by a nominating committee of outside board members. He recommended that a majority of directors be independent rather than company employees. Corporate governance became a popular topic in the business press and for after-dinner speakers.

There has been some movement in the direction of greater independence and responsibility for the board. The ratio of outsiders to insiders on boards has steadily risen. By 1983, 70 percent of directors were outsiders, according to a study by Arthur Young. (Edwin S. Mruk and James A. Giardina, "Organization and Compensation of Boards of Directors.") In 1977, the New York Stock Exchange adopted a rule that in order to be listed, a company would be required to have an audit committee composed exclusively of independent directors. The use of nominating committees of boards to select new directors has become more common. A study by Korn/Ferry International indicated that as recently as 1977, less than 20 percent of the companies polled had such groups whereas the Arthur Young study showed that about 50 percent had them in 1983.

This trend may have slowed. Few directors have been held liable for errors they have made. The general change in tone was reflected in a sharp drop in the rates for directors' and officers' insurance in the early 80s. The business community successfully resisted SEC

Chairman Williams' proposals. The CEO is still chairman in the vast majority of large corporations. The rules of the game still apply.

The opposition of the business community to proposed reforms is not based entirely on the interest of CEOs to maintain their freedom of action. There are practical problems with some of the ideas that have been put forth. For example, I have served as chairman of a company in which the company president was CEO and found the arrangement to be a bit awkward. Recognizing potential difficulties in that situation, I put top priority on maintaining an open, constructive relationship with the CEO. In hindsight, I believe I might have contributed more by being more forceful.

Nevertheless, it still appears to me that on balance, companies would do well to separate the positions of CEO and chairman of the board. Having an independent chairman setting agendas, specifying what information should be provided to directors, and stimulating needed board action on strategy and policies could have a salutary effect on corporate performance.

Most companies conduct a performance review at least annually for every executive except the CEO. This provides the individual with information on how his progress is regarded by his superiors and points out for him the areas in which he should strive for improvement. Rarely is the CEO given such an opportunity. Directors shy away from that kind of activity. The CEO is left to look for indirect signs and to try to interpret them. Informal meetings of two or more directors in his absence can have an ominous connotation. As a consultant, I have had occasion to ask a number of CEOs about whether they felt their jobs were secure and have been surprised at how uncertain they were about what their boards thought of them.

The CEO of an American corporation is in a position something like that of the dictator of a nation. He has enormous power but is vulnerable to being ousted suddenly if things go badly.

An arrangement in which the board provided more supervision and guidance for the CEO would be an improvement over what we normally have. The objectivity and experience of capable, independent directors would foster greater management vision. The CEO would have a better idea of what was expected of him and how well he was doing. There would be less chance of the company being led to disaster by an incapable or irresponsible chief executive.

Such a system would require an ample supply of independent directors who would be willing and able to fill their roles. In fact, few directors are prepared to do so. Some lack the ability. Some are concerned about personal risk. Some would not be willing to spend the needed time. Still others would, as they do now, act primarily to further their own private interests. Most would feel uncomfortable undertaking to supervise the CEO.

A more immediate question is what agent of change is available to affect how boards perform. Most executives seem satisfied with the status quo. Those who see the need for change don't see what they can do to bring it about. Even the head of the SEC was unable to have much impact when he campaigned for reform in corporate governance. And as he said, it seems unlikely that government regulation would have any salutary effect.

Progress, if it is to continue, will come from increased awareness of the need for improvement. When companies blunder and write off hundreds of millions, when American industry loses its competitive edge, when corporations pay greenmail, and when boards pile outlandish golden parachutes on top of already lavish executive compensation programs, people see that something is wrong with the way corporations are governed. They see the need for change.

Already, strong voices are calling for a national industrial policy under the leadership of the U.S. government. They are calling for new laws to prevent abuses such as greenmail and golden parachutes. They are calling for increased personal liability for directors.

A better alternative is for the business community itself to respond voluntarily to the need for greater responsibility and improved performance by boards of directors. CEOs can make better use of their boards when they formulate strategy and set long range plans. Directors can assert their authority more vigorously to keep corporate action consistent with the objectives of all interested parties. By insisting on sound game plans, they can improve corporate performance and our overall economic effectiveness.

# PART 2

# DEVELOPING YOUR GAME PLAN

# 6

# Defining Your Business

"The objective of this company is to make a profit. We will do whatever promises to make a buck provided only that it is legal and ethical." Thus do many chief executives define their businesses. Such a definition provides no direction as to where to look for opportunities. It affords no guidance as to what resources and capabilities to develop for the long run. It ignores the question of how to win a lasting competitive advantage or to generate some sort of fundamental reason to expect good results. It represents a policy of opportunism.

Such a philosophy lies behind the actions of many companies. It has led many a corporation to acquire businesses in which it had no experience and was not well qualified. We have seen how Beatrice Foods, Gulf & Western, Warner Communications, and the big oil companies lost hundreds of millions each by investing in operations outside their areas of competence. Large as these figures are, they pale by comparison with the collective losses incurred by thousands of firms that continue to invest in products, services, and markets offering no reasonable prospect of attractive returns.

Success in any undertaking depends on having the right capabilities and tools. One doesn't hunt elephants with a pea-shooter nor mosquitoes with a meat-axe. One must match his resources to his undertaking. In an enterprise, management must define the business so as to achieve an effective matchup as indicated in Chart 1-1 on page 6.

A sound business definition directs a company's resources toward activities in which it can become better qualified than its competitors. It provides managers with guidelines for determining

65

which market segments to pursue and which capabilities to develop. It represents a basis for expecting to achieve an attractive return on capital. Without such a definition to light the way, companies stumble forward in the dark, run with the herd, or pursue new opportunities based on little more than determination and hope.

A sound business definition aims at filling real economic needs. If a company develops a distinctive competence to fill well-defined needs, it has a sound basis for expecting to do well financially. But if it pursues profits more superficially and opportunistically, it is likely to have trouble earning an attractive return in the long run. Similarly, if in serving its customers, it damages the environment or otherwise harms society, it will be on thin ice. The public through its government continues to find new ways to make industry pay for the damage it does. Many businesses that showed a profit when they didn't have to pay for degrading the environment, or when they manufactured unsafe products, were unable to survive when new laws and regulations were imposed.

A sound business definition does not necessarily require a formal procedure or written document. Many companies, especially smaller ones, produce outstanding results without any formal system at all. For example, the proprietor of a successful small printing company near Boston defined his business precisely. He pinpointed the geographical area he would serve, the quantities he would sell, the kind of equipment he would use, and the specific types of customers he would seek. He did this informally, without committing any of it to writing.

Other companies, especially larger ones, prepare elaborate strategic plans, codes of ethics, and statements of mission, policies, and philosophy but fail to integrate their activities into sensible strategic programs. Many of their pompous pronouncements are pure nonsense and contribute nothing to the economic progress of the business. What counts is not form but substance.

The definition of the business is top management's vision of what a company is and what it will do. It is comprised of three major elements:

1. The general nature of the enterprise.
2. The business areas in which it will operate: which customers it will serve, which of their needs it will fill, and how.
3. The specific capabilities and resources it will develop to achieve a competitive edge.

## GENERAL NATURE

If one buys from a company, sells to it, or especially if one is employed by it, he quickly gets an idea of its general nature. He sees it in the appearance of the place, in the attitudes of the employees, in the way they relate to one another, and in their level of competence.

In some firms, employees work enthusiastically together to serve their customers. In others, they are surly to clients and are at each others' throats. In some companies, workers pay attention to detail, keep things neat, and operate efficiently. In others, people are sloppy, wasteful, dirty. Some seem to pinch every penny while others spend money with wild abandon. Some seek to use the most modern technology while others cling to proven ways.

Management practices have an important effect on a company's general nature. Some go in for formality and keep up to date on the latest management techniques. They maintain procedures manuals, organization charts, and job descriptions. Others are able to get the job done with less fuss. For example, in one successful small company the key executives shared a single crowded office. It was impossible for any of them to have a private conversation. Communication and coordination between them was outstanding!

The nature of a company affects what it can do well. Some companies have a collegial atmosphere in which new ideas are encouraged and respected. Such firms may be well suited for businesses in which innovation is important such as publishing, advertising, or high-technology manufacturing. Other firms, characterized by iron discipline and control, do better in more mature, stable environments. Attitudes toward quality, costs, or special customer needs are often critical to what a firm can or cannot do well.

Exxon's problems in diversification, for example, relate to the general nature of the company. It has a management culture appropriate to its role as a giant multinational oil corporation. With a net worth of tens of billions and sales of scores of billions, its decisions involve enormous amounts of money. Such choices require thorough study and analysis. This pattern of slow, careful decision making is embedded in its corporate culture. In its own industry, Exxon has been an outstanding success.

In recent years, Exxon has invested billions outside of the oil industry. It spent one billion to acquire Reliance Electric and hundreds of millions more to enter the electronic office automation business. In the electronics industry, however, things change rapidly. A pattern of slow, careful decision making doesn't work. A late decision is a poor one, no matter how accurate the analysis. The result has been that Exxon, a very well-managed enterprise, has been unable to make a profit in electronics. Overall, its diversification led to losses of $700 million over a 10-year period.

Kennecott experienced a similar problem after it acquired Carborundum Co. As Business Week reported on May 23, 1983, "Kennecott's leaders were accustomed to a long analysis of a few major investment decisions. In contrast, an action-oriented top management at Carborundum exerted tight control, but gave line managers great leeway on decisions."

Whether deliberately or by accident, top management influences the culture of an enterprise. By example, by direction, by its system of rewards and punishments, and by its selection of personnel, management shapes the corporate value system, agenda, and culture. In some companies, subordinate executives pattern their clothing, drinking habits, leisure activities, and even patterns of speech after those of the CEO. Observing them in action can be more entertaining than a farce at the theater.

Corporate culture is difficult to change. Even over an extended period of time during which there may be a complete turnover of personnel, corporations tend to maintain the same style. When a new CEO arrives on the scene, the organization resists change. The employees learn how to manage their new boss, to subvert his plans, to get *him* to adopt *their* culture. This is one of the reasons that turnarounds of unsuccessful companies are so difficult.

## BUSINESS AREAS

The second element of a business definition is the specific market segments a company will undertake to serve. Every customer and each of his needs is at least slightly different from all others. But it is not normally practical to offer each buyer a custom-designed product or service that is ideal for him in every way. While some businesses can tailor their offerings considerably to cater to individual customer's needs, it is usually necessary to standardize at least some aspects of their offerings for *groups* of customers. These groups represent segments of a market. Each segment is different from the others.

There is no limit to the number of ways customers can be classified. Geography, price level, quality level, industry, size, amount used, need for service or credit, and responsiveness to various types of sales promotion are only a few of the many criteria that can be used. One can orient his offering to rural customers or urban ones, to ethnic minorities, to yuppies or golden agers, to large industrial accounts or small ones, to sailors, skiers, dog owners, or equestrians, to Asian immigrants or members of the DAR, to small law firms or large hospitals.

The essential point is that a market segment is not an objective real thing like a dog or a tree. It is an arbitrary grouping of customers done for the convenience and benefit of the supplier.

A company does not have to accept the usual way an industry segments its markets. Automobiles, for example, are usually categorized by size and price. But Volvo characterizes its cars as long-lasting and addresses a segment that values durability. Some cars are designed for sportsmen for use off-the-road. People pay extraordinary prices for custom-built classics. In London, there is a market for taxicabs that are strikingly different from private cars. An automobile company can define its markets in any way it chooses. Its objective is to define market segments in such a way as to secure a potentially telling competitive advantage for itself.

In the past, markets were customarily defined by product. People talked about markets for food, personal computers, or perhaps health care. Then they began adding to the definition the customer type as the institutional food market, the commercial market for personal computers, or health care for private individuals. In his book *Defining the Business* (Prentice-Hall, 1980), Derek Abell proposed defining markets by customer type, the need to be filled, and the way it is filled. One could define an institutional market for precooked, portion-controlled meals, a market for microcomputer systems for value-added resellers (VARs), or a market for walk-in health care for individuals needing minor surgery. For each of these definitions one might include a technical approach or distribution channel specifying *how* the need is to be filled.

With imagination, almost any company can define market segments in which it can reasonably expect to build a competitive edge. How well it defines the segments it will serve can have a great deal to do with the result it achieves.

## RESOURCES AND CAPABILITIES

The third element of a business definition is the specific resources and capabilities on the basis of which a company expects to gain a competitive advantage. These could include location, patents, technical know-how, reputation, economies of scale, distribution channels, relationships, financial strength, or any of a wide variety of other factors. A more subtle resource is the way a company approaches problems and makes decisions.

The relative effectiveness of a supplier in serving customers depends primarily on its capabilities. In some market segments, the most experienced producers with greatest economy of scale may have a decisive advantage as General Motors has had in automobiles or Dow Chemical in chlorine and caustic. In others, technical expertise, specialized products, or a marketing approach geared to the needs of a specific customer group determine which supplier is preferred. Thus Wendy's, Hewlett-Packard, and Saks-Fifth Avenue can succeed in industries dominated by others.

A capability that represents a strength in one area nearly always represents a weakness in others. For every capability there is an associated cost to build and maintain it. For example, a dedication to outstanding quality usually involves a sacrifice in cost. Conversely, concentration on reducing cost can affect quality. Unusual responsiveness to customers' needs costs money in training and manpower. Even a resource such as great financial strength is usually associated with high overheads. Huge corporations such as GE assiduously avoid competing in areas where their financial strength is not needed. They recognize that there is a cost associated with size and that smaller competitors will have an advantage over them in markets in which financial strength isn't required.

Thus an advantage in serving one group of customers represents a disadvantage in trying to serve others. Shoulder pads are necessary in a football game but would not help in a tennis match. A Tiffany image attracts the carriage trade but scares away the bargain hunters. A factory capable of making standard products at minimum cost may not be able to serve customers wanting short-run specials. A retailer catering to patrons who demand a range of choices and extensive after-sale service will not be able to meet the needs of those who buy on price.

This does not imply that there is a neat one-to-one inverse relationship between these pairs of characteristics under all circumstances. Consider quality and cost, for example. Additional internal quality-assurance measures sometimes produce better quality at the same time they lower costs by reducing rework and scrap. New production systems pioneered by the Japanese and new computer-controlled equipment are making it possible to produce a wider variety of products with little sacrifice in cost. Nevertheless, trade-offs between cost and quality and between cost and run length still exist. Especially when the entire system including marketing, development, and financial control are considered, it is clear that the economics of serving a mass market are different from those associated with custom-designed specials.

The relative importance of different capabilities varies widely depending on the specific customer need to be filled. For some buyers, price dominates. For others, quality, convenience, or special features are critical. When one needs a loaf of bread or pint of cream in a hurry, store location determines where he will buy. But when he does his weekly grocery shopping, price, quality of the food, or the ambiance of the store becomes more important. In each market segment, one, two, or at most three factors tend to be the primary influences on buying decisions.

Management decisions determine the capabilities in which a company will develop a competitive advantage. This is done in two ways. One is by spending money specifically to develop capabilities such as a technological competence, a higher quality standard, or a more effective marketing program. The second is by selecting the areas in which the company is active. Simply by serving a market a firm learns to know and understand it. This enhances its ability to design products for it and sell to it. By running certain production operations, a corporation gains know-how in that kind of manufacturing. By focusing activities, a company can expect to excel. By diversifying, it develops a broader range of capabilities but in less depth. Thus by its allocation of expenditures and by its selection of activities, management develops the unique array of capabilities on which its competitive position will depend.

## RELATING COMPANIES TO MARKETS

The process of defining a business is illustrated graphically in Chart 6–1. Management defines the business in terms of the market segments a company will address, the company's character and culture, and its capabilities and resources. Its culture influences the quality and intensity of effort by its employees. Its capabilities and resources determine its relative competitive position: whether it has basic advantages over its rivals. Together, effort and competitive position determine how well the firm serves its customers and what kind of return on invested capital it produces.

**CHART 6–1**

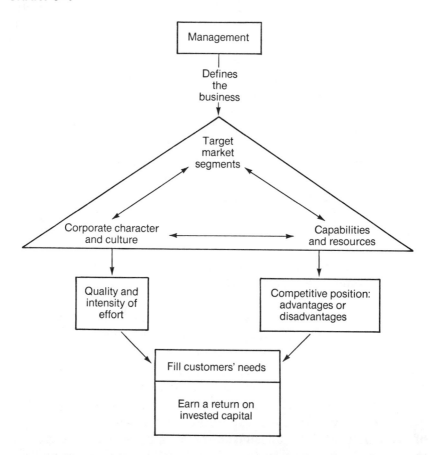

Combining the three elements of the business definition shown in the triangle in Chart 6–1 into a coherent strategy is a key to success. The three elements are interrelated, each depending on the other two. The corporate culture together with its capabilities and resources determine which market segments the firm should address. The market segments it pursues influence the corporate culture and dictate the capabilities management must develop if it is to succeed. The culture of the company helps define its capabilities just as the capabilities help define its culture. A marketing-driven business will be quite different from one in which technical competence is the key determinant of success.

Management vision is needed to match corporate capabilities and culture with the needs of different kinds of potential customers. It is a matter of pegs and holes of different shapes with one major difference. It is easy to see that the square peg won't go into the round hole. But an industrial mismatch, such as Texas Instruments trying to market consumer products, is less obvious and can be much more expensive. In the case of Texas Instruments' home computers, the loss in 1983 alone was $660 million.

Matching a company's competence to market segments has many dimensions. It can involve simply determining the kinds of uses for which a product line is technically appropriate; or it can involve subtler concepts such as identifying customer groups for which a company's style or cost structure is especially appropriate. We saw in Chapter 1 how Chase Brass and Nucor profited by defining their markets and tailoring their capabilities to specific customer groups. The *Fortune* article in the box beginning on page 74 tells how Family Dollar Stores carefully defined its business and built a distinctive competence to serve its targeted market better than any competitor could. Each of these companies built an outstanding record in a highly competitive industry.

## COMPATIBILITY

When a company defines its business, it may have opportunities to gain a competitive advantage by applying an area of competence to several market segments. If its markets are more extensive than its competitors, it can spread its fixed costs over a broader base. It can achieve economies of scale not only in manufacturing but in marketing and engineering as well.

At the same time, companies must consider the compatibility of the various markets they serve. Each customer has different needs. A product line appropriate for one segment is inappropriate for another. A sales force equipped to sell one group of customer is less able to sell others. A product line appropriate for one segment is inappropriate for another. Thus it is that a company such as Ennis Business Forms can be so successful selling in small towns while giant competitors clobber them in the big cities and in large corporate accounts. When a company defines its business too broadly, it finds itself addressing incompatible market segments.

This is represented graphically in Chart 6–2. An industry is composed of many different types of customers. Shown at the center of each circle are large consumers that buy standard products on a highly competitive basis. Around it are other important segments that require a certain amount of special attention. On the fringes are much smaller segments that have unusual requirements

## THE GREEN IN BLUE-COLLAR RETAILING

When they scout sites for new Family Dollar stores, the company's real estate experts look for oil spots and cheap shoes. "Our customers drive old cars that drip a lot of oil," explains company president Lewis Levine. Adds Doug Sullivan, vice president for real esatte: "And we look real hard at shoes because footwear, not clothes, is the giveaway. Lots of people wear old clothes and $50 running shoes. Those are not our customers. We have got to be in low- and lower-middle-income areas."

The family income of a typical Family Dollar customer rarely exceeds $17,000 a year. That's $7,580 below the U.S. median, but it translates into above-average earnings for Family Dollar Stores Inc. By refusing to stray from its lower-income sales strategy, Family Dollar has become one of the most profitable discount retailers. Its 6.9% return on sales of 377 million over the past four quarters was one of the highest among discounters. "Over the last ten years," crows Family Dollar's 1984 annual report, "the compound annual rate of growth was 21% in sales, 32% in earnings . . . [and] 22% in book value per share of common stock."

Family Dollar is little known outside the Southeast, where it operates 889 stores in 20 states from its headquarters in Charlotte, North Carolina. But that may be changing. The company recently opened its first stores in Texas, Missouri, Indiana, Delaware, and New Jersey. By year-end, it intends to have found enough oil spots and cheap shoes to open 100 more stores. Eventually Family Dollar wants to operate stores nationwide. This year's expansion program, plus a $9-million addition to the Charlotte distribution center and warehouse, will be financed entirely by cash; Family Dollar has no debt.

The discounter from North Carolina has pounced on the lower end of the market with a rigid but successful formula: small self-service stores offering merchandise of reasonable quality at low prices. Most items cost $16.99 or less; the average customer spends little more than $6 each trip. All sales are in cash, since Family Dollar has no charge accounts and accepts no credit cards. Stores are virtually identical, cut from a mold carefully crafted at the main office. Each is brightly lit, air-conditioned, well swept, and no larger than 8,000 square feet. About 30% of Family Dollar merchandise carries a brand name. Most of the rest has a manufacturer's label; less than 4% are seconds or irregulars.

Family Dollar slips neatly between its two main competitors in discount retailing: Dollar General at the low end and Wal-Mart at the high. The big attraction at Dollar General (1984 sales: $480 million) is super-low prices, even lower than Family Dollar's. Dollar General has 1,333 stores, also mostly in the Southeast. Half its clothing is either closeouts or irregulars. Wal-Mart, the nimble gorilla of discount retailing, had 1984 sales of $6.4 billion. But Wal-Mart has lately shifted strategy to appeal to more affluent customers, partly to challenge K mart, the nation's largest discount retailer (1984 sales: $21 billion). From garden supplies and cat litter to exercise equipment and stereos, Wal-Mart stocks 60,000 items, spreading them out in stores that cover over an acre. Courting the more well-to-do customer is a growth strategy common to Wal-Mart, K mart, and other discounters. It has helped Wal-Mart push up sales 12% to 15% at most stores in the past couple of years.

With its firm blue-collar fixation and only 5,000 items to choose from, Family Dollar cannot expect to grow as fast. Its stores are rooted in rural areas (more than half are in communities with populations under 15,000), approach their maximum sales potential in the first year, and grow slowly after that. For the fiscal year that ended last August, Family Dollar squeezed a 9% average growth in sales, a six-year high, out of stores open more than one year—what retailers call "same store" growth. For the six months that ended February 28, same- store sales grew at an annual rate of only 3%. Lewis Levine attributes the falloff to the Southeast's unusually mild winter; Family Dollar's customers didn't buy winter clothes as usual.

The company's relatively meager same-store sales growth means it must keep opening new stores to maintain its success. But rapid expansion can be perilous. As Family Dollar moves out of familiar terrain in the Southeast, it may have trouble replicating the formula that has produced 39 straight quarters of record sales and earnings. So far Wall Street doesn't seem worried. Security analyst Skip Helm of William Blair & Co. raves about the company's "superb execution and professional management."

He's referring to Lewis Levine, 51, Lewis's cousin Leon Levine, 47, and Leon's 26-year-old son, Howard. Leon, or Mr. L. as many employees call him, is the chairman, chief executive officer, and founder of Family Dollar. At 12, when his father died, Leon helped his mother manage a small clothing store in rural North Carolina. "I didn't like having a lot of items," he says. "It was too much to keep up with. And we had no charge accounts or credit cards then either. In a small town, if people don't pay their charge accounts there is not very much you can do about it."

Twenty-five years ago, Leon called on his childhood experience to open the first Family Dollar store. He began with $6,000 of his own money. (His stock is worth about $141 million today.) By the late 1960s Family Dollar had grown to 12 stores, and Leon asked Lewis to join the business. Leon still directs Family Dollar from his rosewood desk in a neat and elegant office. But he leaves day-to-day management to Lewis, whose disheveled office reflects his style. Mr. Lewis, as employees call him, is not often behind his desk. "I like to roam," he says, shifting in his chair. "I like to poke into things and I do not like surprises." Mr. Lewis minimizes surprises by imposing unusually close direction from headquarters and taking inventory at 5% of his stores each week. That means each store averages better than 2½ inventories a year; most discount retailers take inventory once a year.

Howard Levine, the heir apparent, has been in the business since the age of 17. He runs the chain's merchandising, advertising, and distribution. Twelve buyers, including his 24-year-old sister, Lori, report to him. "We do not sell fashion," he says. "It doesn't matter to us whether miniskirts are in or out. We sell basic skirts in basic colors. It is our competition that keeps going upscale and all they have done is left us a bigger gap to fill. We do not want to be like Wal-Mart, where you have to walk 40 yards to find something and then wait in long lines to pay for it."

At Family Dollar sales are divided about equally between what the industry calls soft goods (generally anything you wear) and hard goods (pretty much anything you don't). The stores tend to make more money on pants, shirts, and dresses than on toothpaste, bleach, and motor oil. An expensive item at Family Dollar is a $20 electric fan or a 9-by-12 rug that costs $30. Most stores take in a surprisingly consistent $500,000 to $550,000 a year. Fewer than ten ring up $1 million a year in sales.

According to the basic floor plan plotted in Charlotte, women's wear at Family Dollar stores is to the right of the front door, since most customers are women and most shoppers walk to the right when they enter a store. Toys are usually in the back right corner, to draw traffic through the store. Sale items sit strategically at the ends of aisles, normally good impulse-purchase territory.

Each week the chain puts ads in 800 newspapers, many with names that call from another era (*Elba Clipper, Choctaw Advocate, Jeff Davis County Ledger*). At least a dozen times a year it sends out eight million promotional fliers. Conceived and designed at headquarters, they are the same in every area. The company has moved into direct mail because Family Dollar shoppers are not regular newspaper subscribers.

The chain ships all merchandise from a single warehouse at headquarters and sets all prices and markdowns in Charlotte too. Such chainwide uniformity helps Family Dollar keep costs low and makes it easier to manage the stores. That job usually falls to women, high school graduates, many of whom earn no more than their customers: $15,000 to $20,000 a year for a workweek that sometimes stretches to 70 hours. The best managers are eligible for bonuses of $800 to $2,800, based on the performance of their outlets. Lewis Levine says a good manager can improve sales simply by keeping the store clean, the merchandise stacked where it should be, and the price and promotional signs up. "You do not have to be a merchant to run a Family Dollar store," he says.

The Charlotte headquarters "forces" 60% of the merchandise on every store—that is, the Levines, not the manager, decide how much of an item a store will carry. Managers order the quantities of the other 40%, but even those decisions are carefully circumscribed by headquarters. Labels on the shelves, which contain a computerized identification code for each product, plus its name and price, carry tiny numbers that tell a manager the minimum and maximum number of the item that the store should stock.

Family Dollar's frequent inventory taking helps keep theft, or "shrink," to 1.5% of sales, about average for the industry. So, presumably, does the annual lie detector test that all employees must take. "I take it too," says Lewis, a bit uncomfortable with the subject. "We are a team here and the lie detector test makes everyone feel part of the team. Look, most people are basically honest. They just need a little help sometimes."

The Levines' team is certain to get bigger in the next five years. Although security analysts think Family Dollar's same-store growth will probably run around 5% a year, they predict sales and earnings will keep growing 20% to 25% a year as the company opens new stores.

Retailers note, however, that chains seem to hit a wall as sales approach the half-billion-dollar mark. That's the point beyond which expansion programs most often go awry, beyond which there are more frequent surprises. Though all Family Dollar stores now sell the same mix of products, the company will inevitably need to adapt to seasonal needs and regional preferences as its outlets move north and west. And as the Levines expand, they will need to take extra care bringing on new managers. Hiring is always an art, and many rapidly expanding businesses have found to their horror how destructive even a few poorly chosen managers can be.

Along with increasing the number of stores, industry analysts say, the Levines will have to squeeze more sales and profits from existing ones. This may mean adding more merchandise. The trick will be to do that while keeping prices low.

Family Dollar executives realize that growth could be a problem. But they are firm in their conviction that they have the systems in place to become a national chain. "Our strength is that we know this business well," says Leon. "I like the direction of this company and I like it that we do one thing. That means we can identify a problem quickly, that we know how to solve it."

So far Family Dollar hasn't had many problems. It has not guessed wrong on many store locations; in the past 15 years the company has closed only 22 outlets. But as the pressure to expand continues and the company moves into new territories, the danger is that the real estate scouts will forget their primary mission: to keep looking for oil spots and cheap shoes.

SOURCE: Steve Lawrence, "The Green in Blue-Collar Retailing," *Fortune*, May 27, 1985, pp. 74–77. © 1985 Time, Inc. All Rights Reserved.

for which they pay a substantial premium. The differentiation between segments can be by technology, customer size, quality level, product features, geography, or a wide variety of other possible criteria.

Suppliers normally seek to serve as broad a base as they can. Managers with vision strive to identify groups of customers for which their particular capabilities will have the greatest value and to avoid trying to serve markets with needs that are too diverse.

Ways of grouping segments in business definitions are suggested in illustrations *b, c, d, e,* and *f* in Chart 6–2. Definition *b* focuses on standards sold to a variety of customer types. Definition *c* uses a different criterion such as a special type of technology or location to sell a wider variety of customer types and sizes. Definition *d* focuses on the ability to cater to the special needs of many smaller users. Definition *e,* typical of many industry leaders, may include incompatible segments and render the company vulnerable, as in the third of the examples described below. Finally, definition *f* suggests serious incompatibility of targets and probable difficulty in achieving satisfactory results.

**CHART 6–2**

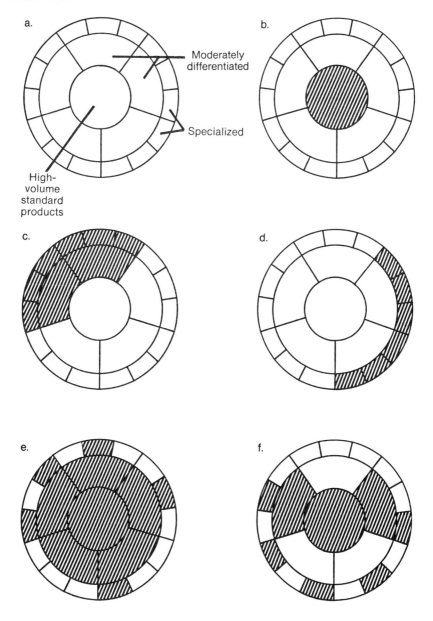

## EXAMPLES

My first job was as a product manager at the Norton Company, the world's largest abrasives manufacturer. Because its raw materials were resistant to high temperatures, it made refractory products as well. My area was kiln furniture: shelves and posts used to support "green" ceramic products that were being fired in kilns to impart hardness and durability.

At that time, Norton was doing poorly in kiln furniture. Its products often failed in use, sometimes causing expensive accidents in customers' plants. Norton's share of the market was a mere 7 percent. After visiting many of the customers with the salesmen, I was discouraged. We had more failures than successes. The salesmen were reluctant to try to sell to new prospects, fearing what the result might be. Yet we still had a few steady customers who were well satisfied with our products.

When our annual sales meeting approached, my boss called me into his office. He realized that I was negative about our situation, but he told me that I must not exhibit that attitude at the sales meeting. Somehow I must find something positive to say to encourage the salesmen.

It was a dilemma. I couldn't lie. Moreover, if I succeeded in getting the salesmen to solicit new customers, we could only expect more failures. That wouldn't help anyone. What was I to do?

Somehow I hit upon the idea of relating the performance of our products to conditions in the customers' plants. I had systematically accumulated and cataloged extensive information about customers' kilns. Two of the important factors in firing ceramics are the amount of heat treatment given and the time required. I drew a graph locating each customer kiln according to those two characteristics. Those who were Norton customers, I colored green, the others red. Lo and behold, there were two clusters of green dots, one for each of the two refractory compositions of our kiln furniture! The graph showed clearly the kinds of kilns in which our products would perform well and where they would not.

At the sales meeting, I showed the graph to the salesmen. With the insight it provided, they gained confidence that they could sell their products for use in certain types of kilns. They avoided the others. By defining our business in straightforward technical terms, we were able to double our share to 14 percent within one year!

A more complex situation involving a wider range of considerations is illustrated by the experience of Citytrust Bancorp, a small bank in Bridgeport, Connecticut. In the 1970s it engaged in a wide range of banking activities. It offered an array of services to many types of commercial accounts as well as to individuals. Results were poor. By 1975, the bank was in trouble. The board fired the chairman and brought in a number of new executives with experience outside the banking field.

The new management decided that the bank's capabilities were best suited to serving smaller companies in its local area. It began focusing on industrial customers with sales in the $1–$25 million range and built specialized capabilities for serving that market segment. It stopped seeking business from corporate giants in nearby New York City. The new CEO said he would fire any employee soliciting business from one of the Fortune 500 companies. The bank also abandoned most of its consumer business. Over the next six years, its earnings increased at a rate of 25 percent annually!

Industry leaders often have trouble competing with a smaller firm, such as Citytrust Bancorp, that focuses on specialized fringe areas of the market. Moreover, when larger corporations define their businesses too broadly, they may become vulnerable to attack at the very heart of their markets, too.

A manufacturer of industrial supplies, the largest in the world in its line, provided a case in point several years ago. It sold a broad line of products to a wide range of users. To reach them all, it used a network of stocking distributors and dealers which maintained large inventories to be able to provide speedy deliveries.

Over a period of years, industry association figures indicated that this company was steadily losing market share. Continuing competitive pressure on prices kept earnings lower than they had once been. Despite intensive efforts to reduce manufacturing costs, develop new products, and improve marketing effectiveness, this firm's position continued to decline. Moreover, it was unable to achieve the kind of return on investment often associated with having the dominant position in an industry.

Ultimately, the company, with the help of outside consultants, uncovered its basic problem. It found that small regional producers were capturing an increasing share of the market by concentrating on the largest users of the most standard products. By limiting their product lines and by manufacturing them in "focused factories," they achieved lower production costs. By selling direct to only a few large users, they reduced marketing costs to almost nothing. Their expenses for R&D, product development, inventories, advertising and sales promotion, and technical service were lower than those of the industry leader. They were able to generate an excellent return on capital at the same time they were increasing their market share by cutting prices. By defining its business too broadly, the top company had exposed itself to competition it could not cope with even at the heart of its market.

## VISION VERSUS EFFORT

Vision affects how different executives evaluate the two factors in Chart 6–1 that determine how well a firm serves its customers.

From the point of view of many operating executives, the key issue is effort. Middle managers have less control over the more basic competitive factors, which in any case usually take years to change. So they focus their attention on motivating their employees to work harder and smarter to cut costs, to sell more aggressively, to operate more effectively. They exhibit the typical symptoms of management myopia.

Executives with vision think differently. They see that in the long run, building basic capabilities and resources will have a more profound effect on results. So they focus their attention on deciding where to compete and what strengths to build.

It is something like an athletic competition such as running. To a casual observer, it appears that the runner who tries hardest wins. But the runners themselves know that much more is involved. Their training program is critically important. And perhaps more important still is selecting the right event. A chunky, heavily muscled person may do well in the dashes but is unlikely to excel in long distances. The thin, wiry build is better for the marathon. Picking the right arena in which to compete and building the particular abilities for that particular event counts for more than effort in the race itself.

The three examples presented above illustrate how performance depends on how well a company's capabilities match up with customer needs. Norton's market position doubled when it learned where its products would work. Citytrust Bancorp was able to develop competitive advantages when it targeted small accounts and abandoned markets for which others were better qualified. By trying to serve too broad a range of customers, the industrial supply manufacturer lost its ability to serve major users as well as smaller competitors could.

Often, companies fail to see that they have defined their businesses in such a way that they are unlikely to achieve favorable results. They attribute their poor performance to the competitive nature of their businesses or to declining demand. They do not see that their basic problem is strategic. They have failed to develop a game plan that provides a sound reason for expecting to succeed.

In the next chapters, we shall consider how to go about creating a strategy that will work. Chapter 7, Designing the System, describes requirements for an effective strategic planning system and shows how typical procedures can fall short of what is needed. The subsequent chapters deal specifically with formulating strategy, planning for the long term, and establishing financial policies.

# 7

# Designing the System

The chairman of a moribund New York Stock Exchange corporation was concerned about his firm's lack of progress. Some years earlier, he had established an annual strategic planning procedure to find ways to expand. But still the company did not grow. When he examined how the plan was actually being used, he found that its only function was to serve as a starting point in preparing the next plan a year later. Discouraged, he scrapped the corporate planning procedure and told division managers simply to do whatever planning they felt their units needed.

This CEO is not the only one to have been disillusioned by the failure of strategic planning. The sad fact is that the annual planning exercises performed by many companies fail to serve any useful purpose. Many continue the process only for window dressing or in a vain effort to stimulate managers to think strategically.

The practical failures of strategic planning have not gone unnoticed by observers of the business scene. Richard Pascale of Stanford wrote a piece in *Fortune* entitled "Our Curious Addiction to Corporate Grand Strategy," pointing out how well the Japanese have done without formal strategic planning systems. Another *Fortune* article, "Corporate Strategies Under Fire," expressed skepticism as to whether strategic planning has any practical value at all.

The problem is not with the concept of using a strategy and long-range planning to guide corporate decisions. We have seen case after case where sound strategies succeed while short-sighted opportunism leads to trouble. The problem is that management lacks the vision to see how these activities can contribute to corporate success. As a result, the procedures they use are ill-suited to the task. Worse than a waste of time, they are sometimes actually counterproductive.

The problems with typical strategic planning procedures stem from four basic errors:

- Executives confuse strategy formulation with long-range planning. By trying to do both together, they end up doing neither well.
- By arranging for the initial strategic inputs to originate in the operating units, top management shirks its responsibility to provide strong leadership for the corporation.
- Creating a single official version of what is expected to occur over the next several years discourages consideration of alternative possibilities, which are frequently the most important.
- The procedure isolates financial planning from strategy formulation and long-range operations planning. It should be an integral part of the overall planning process.

The requirements for effective strategic planning are outlined in the box on page 86; the shortcomings of the typical strategic planning procedure are outlined in the box on page 87. In this chapter, we shall take a good look at how strategic planning is actually done and how it fails to provide management with the vision it needs in making key decisions. We shall then consider approaches to organization and compensation that can assist in making strategic planning more effective. Finally, we shall review how strategic planning is done in Japan to see what we can learn from the experience there.

In subsequent chapters, we shall look in more depth at strategy formulation, long-range planning, and financial policies. It is primarily through those activities that management can translate its hopes for its business into effective, integrated actions.

## CURRENT PRACTICE

The typical strategic planning procedure is carried out annually during the weeks immediately prior to preparing the operating budget. Because the centerpiece of the plan is a financial projection of the future, executives tend to think of it as sort of a long-term budget. The usual procedure is similar to that used in creating the budget.

## REQUIREMENTS FOR EFFECTIVE
## STRATEGIC PLANNING

1. Understand the different objectives and functions of strategy formulation and long-range planning.
2. Perform the two activities separately:
    a. Formulate strategy at infrequent intervals, free from urgent time pressure.
    b. Prepare long-range plans annually.
3. For strategy formulation:
    a. Know the markets.
    b. Know the competition.
    c. Know the business environment.
    d. Evaluate the company's own capabilities.
    e. Segment the markets.
    f. Define the business.
    g. Communicate the strategy.
    h. Establish an aggressive resource development program.
4. For long-range planning:
    a. Fix the period of the plan.
    b. Identify alternative external scenarios.
    c. Prepare a financial model.
    d. Explore the effects of alternative possibilities.
    e. Evaluate alternative budgets.
    f. Establish a tentative budget.
    g. Revise spending as events unfold.

Corporate staff executives are assigned to lead and coordinate the activity. They outline the procedure, establish a schedule, and specify the facts operating executives must provide. These often include information relevant to strategy such as the size and nature of markets, the competitive situation, strengths and weaknesses, and plans for improving the company's position. The heart of the document is a set of pro forma financial statements covering a period of several years.

Operating executives enjoy the exercise about as much as a 10-year old relishes his first piano recital. They know from experience that the activity will be nonproductive. They resent the time taken away from real work to do it. They fill out the forms with the least amount of thought and effort they feel will get by.

---

### SHORTCOMINGS OF THE TYPICAL STRATEGIC PLANNING PROCEDURE

- Strategy formulation and long-range planning are confused with each other.
- The schedule provides inadequate time for strategy formulation.
- Available information is usually inadequate for strategy formulation.
- Initiative with respect to key strategic decisions is assigned to operating units. Once divisions are committed to their programs independently, it is difficult for the corporate office to integrate them into an effective corporate strategy. Neither the scope of the business nor a reasonable basis for expecting a competitive edge is adequately defined.
- Planning takes the form of a single scenario with inadequate provision for contingencies.
- The quality and quantity of interaction between line and staff is inadequate to achieve an effective consensus.

---

Operating units submit their documents to the corporate office where they are reviewed and consolidated into an overall corporate plan. When the combined projections show inadequate earnings, as they usually do, hurried negotiations take place. Top management presses division managers to reduce projected expenditures or to commit to greater sales volume. What changes are made depends on the attitudes and negotiating skills of the various general managers. Ultimately, decisions get made, the unit projections are reconciled with corporate requirements, and an official long-range corporate plan is issued. In it is a rosy picture of the future representing something between what management thinks will happen and what it would like to achieve. Top management likes to keep the plan on the optimistic side, hoping that will motivate executives to try harder to achieve their projections.

The company then prepares the annual operating budget, which conforms to the first year of the long-range plan. The budget is used to control operations; the long-range plan is filed away. When planning time rolls around again, circumstances have changed so that a new long-range plan is needed.

This process contributes little if anything to the development of strategy. Trying to formulate strategy during the planing operation is like a general trying to plot global strategy in the midst of a pitched battle. Defining a business requires time to accumulate information, to analyze it, to get thoughtful inputs from knowledgeable sources, and to identify and evaluate various alternatives. Attempting to combine strategy formulation with the annual planning exercise insures that it will not get the time nor the attention it deserves.

Planning is not properly done either. The essence of planning is to evaluate various possible courses of action under different assumptions about the future. Giving an official blessing to a single scenario discourages managers from considering more radical possibilities, which often represent the best opportunities or most serious risks. The history of corporate disasters is a history of companies that failed to consider how to deal with potentially unfavorable developments that actually occurred. Most of these possibilities could have been foreseen if management had only taken the trouble to look.

Strategies and plans depend importantly on a company's financial situation. Conversely, a company's financial policies should be integrated with its basic direction, goals, and expectations. Yet financial policy formulation is often done quite separately, almost as an afterthought. A company's attitudes toward financing, capital structure, and dividends are developed separately and often reflect past history and custom more than the firm's evolving needs.

The bottom-up nature of the strategic planning procedure is inappropriate. *Top management* is responsible for determining corporate priorities for, and allocating funds among, various operations. When it invites division executives to propose plans for their operations without clear guidelines, it creates a monster with which it must then do battle. Unit managers, having committed to a course of action and feeling responsibility to their staffs to get corporate backing, fight stubbornly to keep their proposals in tact. The final corporate plan represents a series of compromises which still reflect the uncoordinated sources of the original numbers.

Actually, the procedure results in a counterproductive bias in favor of weaker units. Knowing the corporation's financial performance standards, managers of poorly performing operations feel obliged to submit projections showing improvement. Otherwise, they will have trouble getting financial support for their expansion plans or even keeping their jobs. Managers of stronger units, on the other hand, have little incentive to disclose the full extent of their potential. Projections only moderately above corporate standards suffice to get the funding they require. They are well aware that it is much less painful to exceed projections than to fall short. So the politics of the process work to obscure the extent of the differences between prospects for different divisions. The natural result is overinvesting in weak divisions and failure to exploit fully the best opportunities.

Perhaps the most serious fault of the typical strategic planning exercise is that it lulls top management into a false sense of security. Having performed the annual ritual, they feel they have filled their responsibility for formulating strategy and for long-range planning. But as we have seen, such companies have often failed to define their businesses effectively and may not be prepared for the challenges ahead.

## ORGANIZING THE WORK

To provide for formulating stategy, preparing long-range plans, and establishing financial policies with vision, a company must organize the work properly. Elements involved in designing a strategic planning system are shown in the box on page 90.

The first requirement is to recognize that these tasks are different. Their purposes are different and their procedural requirements are different.

*Strategy* deals with *broad* issues such as: What business should we be in? What capabilities should we develop? Where should we allocate our capital? How should we balance the need to commit resources to developing certain capabilities with the need to maintain adequate flexibility? Formulating or revising basic strategy should be done infrequently. Strategy deals with developing competitive superiority in key capabilities, which takes years. Changes are expensive; vacillation can be disastrous. When strategy must be modified, plenty of time should be allowed to do the job right.

*Long-range planning* deals with *specific* questions such as: How much money will we need? How many people and of what qualifications? When should we expand capacity? What circumstances might lead to running out of money? Long-range planning needs to be done each year or more often if the situation requires. A tight schedule is appropriate.

Financial policies and plans are properly a part of both strategy formulation and long-range planning. A company's financial resources are one determinant of what businesses it should be in and what capabilities it should seek to develop as a basis for its com-

---

**ELEMENTS IN DESIGNING A STRATEGIC
PLANNING SYSTEM**

- Define the different objectives and requirements of strategies, long-range plans, and financial policies.
- Assign responsibility for each function, providing for involving key executives in each.
- Recognize the importance of these activities in the executive reward system.
- Reformulate strategies at infrequent intervals as necessitated by fundamental changes in the situation. Monitor the situation to be able to determine when a change in strategy is needed.
- Allow ample time for properly reformulating strategy when it is done.
- Prepare long-range plans at least annually.
- Establish broad financial policies when corporate strategy is formulated. Incorporate financial plans in the long-range planning exercises.

---

petitive advantage. At the same time, financial considerations must be an integral part of a company's long-range plans.

The CEO is responsible for strategy formulation. Strategic decisions have a major impact on corporate performance over a long period of time. The chief executive can and must involve others to gather and analyze information and to contribute ideas and insights. Ultimately, however, the decision-making responsibility is his.

A company's strategy reflects the CEO's view of the company's economic role and where and how it will outperform others. In considering his alternatives, a good CEO needs peripheral vision akin to those of a basketball player. In addition to what is in front of him, he must be aware of what is going on elsewhere on the court. Satchel Paige, the baseball player, was noted for saying that he never looked back for fear he would see someone gaining on him. For an executive such an attitude would be foolhardy. He cannot afford to ignore what is happening around him while he pursues a plan based on uncertain assumptions.

Because reformulating strategy is not a continuing, routine activity, organizing to get the work done presents special problems.In a complex situation, there is more to be done than the CEO can do single-handedly. Moreover, it is important to have key executives involved in the process so that they will understand the decisions that are made, buy into them, and contribute to their successful implementation. A useful device for these purposes is a *strategy task force*.

The CEO should participate in and normally should direct the work of such a group. Executives in charge of those functions that are the keys to competitive differentiation should be included. In a high-technology company, the head of R&D is needed. In a commodity manufacturing business, the production chief is appropriate. In most companies, the heads of finance and marketing have important contributions to make.

Participating on such a task force affords an opportunity for executives to develop their own strategic vision. Members should be recruited with this in mind.

The tasks involved in strategy formulation are described in Chapter 8. Adequate time, measured in months, should be allowed to get the work done properly. Information will have to be gathered. Diverse opinions should be sought out. A wide range of possibilities including innovative or radical alternatives should be considered.

As issues emerge and the CEO begins to come to conclusions, he should review them with directors. They can often contribute to the CEO's thinking. In any case, their support will be needed in implementing decisions that are made.

Once the corporate strategy is formulated, the CEO must articulate it so that the organization understands and accepts it. Often, it is helpful for competitors to understand it too. If they do, they may be more likely to target other areas for investment. Secrecy is more important with respect to tactical moves.

Business strategies are also needed in the individual operating units. Top management must require that the strategy for each division conform to that of the corporation. When the latter changes, those of the operating units have to be revised as well.

Task forces at the division level can be effective in formulating strategies too. They should contain at least one strong member of the corporate office, sometimes even the CEO, to see that division moves are consistent with the overall corporate program. Moreover, top management must recognize that not all effective operating executives are good strategists. Senior management should provide whatever help each unit needs to develop an appropriate strategy.

The extent to which a division strategy should be dictated by the corporate office depends on the specific situation. Where different units sell to the same customers through similar channels, as in Proctor & Gamble, division strategies and policies must be closely coordinated with each other and with those of the corporation. When a company is entering a new field, it should be open to the use of strategies quite different from ones in its main business. The spectacular success of IBM in the personal computer field derived from the remarkable willingness of top management to allow the PC group to use approaches quite different from those Big Blue used elsewhere. In a case of gross diversification such as Exxon's entry into office electronics, it is essential to refrain from imposing policies and practices based on experience in other fields.

Long-range planning, which needs to be done at least annually, should be coordinated by the corporate office. Responsibility can be assigned either to the finance department or to a planning group reporting to top management. In very small companies, it may be done by the chief financial officer or even by the CEO.

It is important that the corporate coordination be done by people with a keen appreciation for the practical possibilities and constraints of operations. Preferably, the planning department will be staffed by executives with successful operating experience. One of the reasons why Japanese planning operations succeed is that the planners have had line experience.

Financial policies and plans should be reflected in the long-range corporate plans. The broad financial policy included in the strategy needs to be translated into more detailed plans to fit specific situations. Because financial conditions and needs keep changing, plans need to be reviewed at least annually or whenever there are important developments.

The corporation must provide for monitoring its situation to determine when a revision of strategy, long-range plans, or financial policy is needed. Especially because strategy formulation need not be done regularly, it is important to set up a control mechanism to see that strategies are not allowed to become obsolete.

The central responsibility for maintaining the currency of strategies and plans rests with the CEO. He must be aware of what is happening and see when strategies or plans must be revised. Directors, especially if they are encouraged to do so, can raise timely questions about the implications of external or internal developments. An annual strategic planning meeting of senior executives is an excellent forum for considering the adequacy of strategies, plans, and the procedures by which they are developed. Similarly, putting strategy on the board agenda at least once a year can help keep it sound and current. Many companies schedule a special meeting of the board, often at a resort location, for a day or more to consider the basic position and direction of the firm. Usually senior executives also participate in such affairs, exchanging views with directors and working toward consensus on the company's long-term program.

## THE REWARD SYSTEM

If a company expects its executives to do strategy formulation and long-range planning effectively, its reward system must reflect that objective. In American industry today, it rarely does. Executive compensation, recognition, and advancement depend primarily on a manager's contributions to current earnings. Recognizing the problem, some firms have introduced schemes to put more emphasis on the future in their incentive compensation plans. There is, however, a fundamental problem that is seldom adquately addressed.

Incentive compensation is intended to encourage effective *action*. But payments are tied to *results*. Where the two are closely related, that is not a problem. If a salesman makes more calls, organizes his work better, and develops a more persuasive approach, he will sell more. An incentive compensation plan based on his results is likely to stimulate more effective action.

But when it comes to formulating strategy and developing long-range plans, the relationship between action and results is looser and more distant. Earnings in the immediate future, or even over two or three years, are not primarily dependent on how effectively executives set strategy or prepare long-range plans. So incentives based on profitability over even several years provide little incentive to improve today's strategic actions.

We have already noted the weakness of incentive plans tied to the value of company shares. The payoff is highly dependent on market conditions and other circumstances outside of the control of management. Moreover, incentives tied to company stock tend to focus executive attention even more acutely on short-term results because of their effect on the share price.

An alternative is to determine what kind of behavior is desired and to tie incentive compensation to that. At Ventron Corporation, we used such a system successfully for a number of years. Incentive compensation was based on two factors. One was current results. The other was action taken to enhance future earnings, which we called "resource development."

Before the beginning of each year, we identified specific criteria for incentive payment awards that we thought would improve long-term results. Research spending, staff upgrades, organizational development, strategy formulation, long-range planning, and earnings budgeted for the following year are examples of parameters we used. Where possible, we tied performance to objective measurement but did not shrink from qualitative judgment calls. We were pleased with the results.

No system is a panacea. Any compensation plan which appears to demonstrate management's commitment to managing for the long term can be helpful. The message conveyed may be more effective than the expectation of reward itself. A simple, direct approach is likely to be more cost-effective than one involving complex formulas that take years to pay out and are awkward to administer. Poorly designed incentive compensation systems can do more harm than good.

Actually, salary increases and career advancement are reward enough to be effective if they are administered properly. When management bases increases and promotions on criteria employees clearly understand, it can have a powerful effect on motivation. To the extent that actions aimed at long-term results are taken into consideration and employees are aware of that fact, there will be a strong incentive to perform in that area as well as for the short term.

## STRATEGIC PLANNING IN JAPAN

Strategic planning procedures have received less attention in Japan than in the United States. In many ways, the Japanese, who are newer at it, use less sophisticated methods. Like Americans, they often make strategic errors. Yet the usual Japanese approach to strategic planning has features many American companies would do well to emulate.

In Japan, strategy formulation is separated from long-range planning. It is done informally. In some Japanese companies, the general strategic direction reflects a gradual process toward consensus among the management. In others, it is guided primarily by a dominant chief executive.

In either case, from time to time the CEO articulates his basic vision of the future of the business. Such a pronouncement, when it is made, helps shape the company for years to come. It defines the basic policies and spirit of the enterprise and its scope of operations.

Dr. Kobayashi's C&C (Computers & Communications) concept of NEC's future is so important that the company features it not only in its annual report but in its advertising. Every Toyota employee knows that the company specializes in small cars and would never consider making Cadillacs. At Hattori Seiko, the entire management team is working to transform the company according to a concept announced in 1980 by Dr. Hattori. He likened Seiko's present product line to Mount Fuji—as that mountain dominates the Japanese landscape, watches dominate Seiko's operations. By 1990, he envisions an enterprise like Yatsugatake, a famous Japanese mountain with eight peaks. He wants eight product lines built on technologies in which Seiko already has substantial strength. Semiconductors, computers, robots, and instruments have already been identified as areas in which Seiko will grow. Whether going into as many as seven new fields is wise is uncertain, but there is no questions that the people of Seiko are working together to that end.

One of the salient features of any Japanese corporate brochure is a history of the company charted to show the date of each significant step in its progress. Management impresses on its employees a sense of the company's continuity, traditions, direction, and uniqueness. This helps define for the employees where they are headed and how they should move forward. Japanese top managements place great emphasis on their vision of the future and work hard to impress their people with its importance.

The common dedication of Japanese employees to achieving the goals articulated by the head of the company contributes to their extraordinary operating effectiveness. If the American response to the Japanese industrial challenge is limited to operating techniques alone, it will fall short of its goal.

Japanese annual planning seems similar to American procedures, but there are important differences. Japanese companies refer to their plans as intermediate-range rather than long-range. They usually cover three or five years, more often three. The approach is more *top-down* than *bottom-up*.

Members of the planning department conduct a series of discussions with line executives and with senior management before anything is committed to writing. Their aim is to devise a plan that will both implement the CEO's strategic vision for the corporation and also be within the ability of operating units to implement. After thoroughly exploring the subject with all parties involved, the planning department prepares a tentative intermediate-term plan. It represents senior management's view of what the company should expect to accomplish in light of the inputs of operating units. In contrast to the American uncoordinated, bottom-up approach, the first planning numbers committed to paper reflect top management's overall vision of the situation and the future.

Operating units then do the detailed planning needed to determine how to achieve the proposed goals. Planning department executives work with them to help find ways to meet challenging objectives. When appropriate, the counsel of senior executives is solicited. Line managers feel a strong obligation to develop plans that will conform to the original targets. Occasionally they are unable to do so, and the proposed plan must be adjusted. But the starting point from which changes, if any, are made is a coherent, integrated plan.

The strengths of Japanese strategic planning procedures lie in:

- Separation of strategy formulation from long-range planning.
- Emphasis placed on the vision of the corporation's long-term future articulated by the CEO and widely disseminated to the organization.
- The top-down approach to planning.
- The extensive interaction between all concerned parties arranged by planning executives with line experience.
- The meticulous detail of the plans.

These strengths may more than offset more sophisticated American methods such as:

- Conceptual approaches to competitive positioning.
- Quantitative techniques such as internal rate of return, net present value, and computer modeling.
- Reliance on various strategic principles such as diversification.
- Staffing planning units with bright MBAs.

This is not to suggest that Japanese strategic planning is superlative nor even adequate. Even more than American companies, Japanese are obsessed by a compulsion to grow. The visions they follow often fail to define their businesses so as to provide for basic competitive advantages. Japanese companies tend to run with the herd, relying more on intensive effort than on strategic insights for success. Financial planning is largely separated from strategy formulation and long-range business planning. Japanese often rely heavily on outside institutions for guidance in financial policy.

But the basic approach of separating the process of envisioning the basic corporate economic role from the detailed planning operation has served Japanese industry well. American firms would do well to study and to learn from it. The performance of American industry in competition with Japan will depend to a considerable extent on its improving its approach to strategy formulation, long-range planning, and financial policies. Suggested approaches to each of these areas appears in the next three chapters.

# 8

# Formulating Strategy

The word *strategy* is itself a problem. Different people use the word to mean different things. Many books on the subject include a definition of strategy, each different from the others. Some executives have come to use the word simply as a synonym for important. It has been so hackneyed that if there were a reasonable alternative, we would keep the term out of this book altogether. But we have not found a good substitute. Reluctantly, we use the word and include our own definition.

In this book, *strategy* is used to mean a general approach to running a business that can reasonably be expected to achieve superior results. We take the position that simply trying harder to do the same kinds of things in the same ways that competitors do does not represent a reasonable basis for expecting success. That game is simply the old competitive treadmill. Long-term performance is likely to depend more on a company's basic capabilities and resources and the extent to which they are applied to specific market segments where they provide competitive advantage. Thus we use the term strategy to signify a company's definition of its unique economic role, of the capabilities and resources in which it will excel, and of the specific market segments it will address.

A company's strategy guides its decisions about where to allocate capital, how much to invest, which skills and assets to develop, and where to apply them. It is the basis for a company's game plan.

Without a sound strategy, corporations undertake projects that have little likelihood of producing attractive returns or that conflict with other elements of the enterprise. Without a sound strategy,

---

### KEYS TO FORMULATING COMPETITIVE STRATEGY

1. Understand what competitive strategy is and how it works.
2. Focus on practical substance rather than on forms and procedures.
3. Understand the business environment:
   A. The market.
   B. The competitors.
   C. Other factors which affect operations.
4. Recognize the company's own capabilities and limitations.
5. Select market segments in which the company can reasonably expect to excel.
6. Develop resources and capabilities that will afford lasting competitive advantages in these carefully defined market segments.

### BARRIERS TO SUCCESSFUL STRATEGY FORMULATION

1. Failure to understand the function of strategy in promoting competitive success.
2. Preoccupation with form and procedure rather than dealing with content.
3. Lack of information about or understanding of markets or competitors; inability to think in terms of market segments.
4. Concentrating on defeating competitors rather than on building competence to serve customers better.
5. Management myopia.

---

companies fail to invest in assets that would provide basic advantages. They end up facing competitors who are better equipped than they to serve their customers. Under such circumstances, they cannot expect favorable results.

Executives who are preoccupied with operations usually fail to develop effective strategies. This leaves the door wide open for others to develop advantages over them. Without a sound strategy to guide it, a corporation's position is vulnerable to attack by competitors who equip themselves better to serve specific market segments.

A sound strategy can offset shortcomings in operating effectiveness. General Robert Wood, who spearheaded Sears Roebuck's move into retail stores, said that the company "made every mistake in the book" in its retail selling and administration. "Business is like war in one respect," Wood wrote, "If its grand strategy is correct, any number of tactical errors can be made and yet the enterprise proves successful". (Albert D. Chandler, Jr., *Strategy and Structure,* MIT Press, 1962.)

Each business needs a strategy. A diversified corporation needs an overall corporate strategy as well as one for each business unit. While the underlying concepts are similar, the specific issues involved in formulating strategy at the corporate level are different from those at the unit level. This is discussed further in Chapter 13.

## VISION AND COMPETITIVE STRATEGY

Vision is a prerequisite to effective competitive strategy formulation. Management must be able to see its business objectively in relation to its economic environment. It must be able to recognize the strengths and weaknesses in its own organization relative to the needs of specific customer groups. It must accept the fact that there is a limited number of things any company can do well. It must allocate resources only to areas in which it can reasonably expect to excel. It must commit itself to identifying specific market segments for which it can develop a distinctive and superior competence to serve. It must look to superiority in capabilities as its principal competitive weapon. Ideally, management will identify specific areas of competence in which the corporation can build a leading position and that will provide significant advantages to all of its operating units.

Executives with management myopia are unable to formulate meaningful strategies. Their annual strategic planning ritual is about as effective as an Indian rain dance. In practice, a management that places its faith in effort, tactics, and opportunism will ignore strategic guidelines whenever they conflict with short-term considerations. Many companies perform an annual strategic planning exercise only because they feel it is expected of them. In Chapter 7, we saw how such empty procedures not only waste time but can actually be counterproductive.

The futility of trying to formulate strategy without a clear understanding of its situation is sometimes clearly, if inadvertently, displayed by large corporations. In its annual report for 1979, when its common equity was still well over $2 billion, International Harvester wrote about its "significant progress" in that year. "These results represent a significant achievement," it said, "and one that signals International Harvester's potential for greater advances in the future. The 1979 results also confirm that the internal improvement programs now in place are succeeding, even in their early stages, to bring the company's performance closer to its potential." In its 1980 report, one could learn that "International Harvester enters 1981 following a tightly focused, long-term strategy to improve our cost structure, advance IH product and market superiority, and make maximum use of company resources—both human and financial." And, "International Harvester's performance in the last half of fiscal 1980 proved again the basic strengths of this Company and the effectiveness of its long-term strategy." And finally, "Our earning power is unmatched in recent IH history and growing."

Under "Aggressive Strategies for Profitability," the 1981 report included this paragraph:

> In the short term, we are restructuring the Company to break even by the second or third quarters of fiscal 1982, even if markets do not improve by other than normal seasonal patterns as is currently forecast. For the longer term, we are focusing our strengths so as to be profitable in the valleys of future business cycles in the 1980s.

By October 1982, Harvester's common equity had plunged to less than zero. Over the three years covered by these glowing reports, International Harvester had lost over $2.5 billion! If management had any idea about what its situation really was, it certainly was not letting its shareholders know.

A clear vision of a company's condition, its environment, its competitive position, and its opportunities is a prerequisite to formulating a sound game plan. A strategy provides guidelines for decision making based on those factors. It establishes criteria for determining how to allocate money and effort, which customers to pursue, and what capabilities to develop. It translates vision into action.

At the same time, the process of formulating competitive strategy can enhance executive vision. As management accumulates and analyzes data, checks assumptions, and evaluates alternatives, it is looking at basic factors that will determine its future. It is that process of looking broadly at a business and its environment that develops vision.

The essence of formulating competitive strategy is in defining the business, as was discussed in Chapter 6 and illustrated in Chart

---

### ESSENTIAL ELEMENTS OF STRATEGY FORMULATION

1. Know your markets.
2. Know your competitors.
3. Know your business environment.
4. Know your company's own capabilities and limitations.
5. Segment your markets.
6. Define your business.
7. Communicate your decisions to the organization.
8. Establish an aggressive resource development program.

---

6–1. The key elements are shown in the box above. The balance of this chapter discusses practical steps for developing a strategy. What is presented is not a detailed procedure but rather the basic elements needed in the strategy formulation process. *Each company must develop detailed procedures to meet the needs of its own situation.*

The key to effective strategy formulation is understanding what strategy is and how it can contribute to the success of an enterprise. Unless top management is clear about the purpose of the activity, no canned procedure will produce results. Conversely, when a CEO understands what he is about, the procedure he selects is of secondary importance. Many chief executives, especially in smaller firms, devise successful strategies with no formal procedure at all.

A company must allow itself enough time to do the job properly. Trying to perform all these tasks in the few weeks before the annual budgeting exercise is hopeless. Depending on the situation, many months are likely to be needed. Fortunately, major revisions of basic strategy are not required very often. But when management recognizes that the firm needs to reappraise its competitive position and to redefine its business, it should take the time to do the job well. Failing to get at fundamental strategic issues ends up being much more expensive in the long run.

The most important function of a formalized strategy formulation procedure is to provide a check list of tasks to be accomplished and a sensible sequence for doing them. How the work is assigned will depend on how much needs to be done and how the firm is organized. The essential elements required for formulating strategy follow.

## Know Your Markets

Understanding a market goes far beyond statistics on its size, growth rate, and location. A supplier must understand his customers' needs and what affects their buying decisions if he is to win their business. Such knowledge is critically important to decisions about product design, pricing, terms of sale, channels of distribution, and marketing mix as well as to more basic strategic positioning. Information about the size of each segment of the market is necessary for rational decisions about where to allocate resources.

The strategic objective is to build capabilities superior to those of competitors in the specific areas that are most important to the customers. It is essential to understand the markets well enough to identify clearly what those areas are in order to know which specific competitive advantages will produce the greatest results.

Because market knowledge is so essential to success, a company may appoint one or more executives to appraise the adequacy of the firm's information about its markets during the strategy formulation program. A consultant or director can often be helpful here: An objective outsider can often spot weaknesses in a company's understanding of its markets. One way or another, the chief executive must satisfy himself that his company is properly informed. Until it is, efforts at strategy formulation are unlikely to be very productive.

Especially because the need for market knowledge is so widely recognized, it is surprising how little many companies know about their markets. Corporations often undertake expensive product development programs with only the sketchiest information about what they could reasonably hope to sell. One company relied on information from a single potential user when it spent two years to develop a complex, expensive machine. Only when the project was completed and the customer had bought the machine did the developer learn that it had already filled the entire worldwide need for such equipment.

On another occasion, my former employer, the Norton Company, spent nearly a year devising a way to manufacture high-alumina spheres 10 inches in diameter at the specific request of a potential customer. When it showed one of these enormous balls to the prospect, it learned that what he really wanted was $\frac{1}{10}$-inch pellets. Business boners from Ford's Edsel to Texas In-

struments' home computer are usually caused by failure to understand what the customer really wants.

Getting information about markets is straightforward. Being
engaged in a business provides ample opportunity to find out about
customers and their needs. An alert, inquiring company soon learns
a great deal about its markets. Well-managed companies have their
salesmen and whoever else contacts customers systematically record and catalog information about them. One of the key assets of
the large Japanese trading companies that has led to their remarkable success is their ability to collect and use detailed information
about markets on a global scale.

Feedback from customers about product performance, quality,
suitability for the application, and ease of use are invaluable to
product development and manufacturing operations. Marketers can
learn from experience what kinds of promotional activities bring
the greatest response per dollar spent on each type of customer.
Wise managers provide opportunities for development personnel
and executives from other functions to contact customers so that
the whole organization understands their needs and desires. In such
a way, the enterprise can better orient its activities to meeting
customer needs.

When a firm is considering a new activity or recognizes that it
needs more information on its present markets, it can turn to other
sources. The federal government offers a broad array of market
data. Industry associations and trade journals can frequently provide information not only about the size and location of various
segments of the market but also about business practices in the
industry. More detailed information is sometimes available in the
form of multiple-client studies done by consulting firms. When a
company cannot learn enough from existing sources, it can initiate
its own market research project aimed at its specific needs.

Such an investigation can be done either by company personnel
or by an outside contractor. A market research firm may have more
expertise, have special information sources or industry background, and be more objective. However, using outsiders means
educating their people rather than company personnel. When company employees do the work, what they learn and the contacts
they make become corporate assets. Occasioinally, company participation in a project managed by an outside firm can provide
optimum value.

In some cases, the best way to get information about a market
is to test the water. Publishers sometimes announce a book before

it is written and base the decision as to whether to proceed on the response to the announcement. In packaged consumer goods, it is a standard practice to test market a new product in a narrow geographical area before making a major investment in a national advertising and promotional campaign. In many other manufactured goods and services, it is possible to offer a new product on a limited scale to obtain valuable information about the market.

Strategic errors stemming from inadequate understanding of the market can be expensive. Sometimes they are fatal. Useful information on even the most obscure market segments can be developed, usually at a modest cost. Failure to do so is like driving on an expressway wearing a blindfold. One should consider himself lucky if he merely survives.

## Know Your Competitors

A fundamental objective of strategy is to be different from competitors in a way that enables a company to serve at least some groups of customers better than others. To achieve that end, it is essential to understand one's competitors and to know their capabilities and limitations.

Executives often misjudge the competence of their competitors. Especially when considering a new market, they see how far present suppliers are from perfection. But they may overlook the reasons for their apparent shortcomings. More importantly, companies frequently fail to take adequately into account the value of years of experience selling to an industry, of the knowledge about the quirks of the specific market, and of the personal contacts built up over time. Companies often barge into a new field only to find both that doing business there was tougher and that existing suppliers were more competent and resilient than they had realized. We have already cited examples of such errors by American Motors and the regional airlines.

Companies also overestimate the strength of competitors at times. The awesome size of a corporate giant makes would-be rivals quake. Small firms fear irrational price competition because losses in the division with which they compete would be insignificant in the financial results of the giant corporate parent. With few exceptions, big companies don't operate that way. Division behavior reflects the interests of the unit management, which has plenty of incentive to earn money not only every year but every quarter. Only when a corporation has some very special reason for building its entry in a particular industry will it countenance sacrificing earnings by deliberate underpricing. Nearly every industry includes successful smaller participants. We have already cited a number of examples of small companies such as Nucor and Citytrust Bank-corp that do very well in industries dominated by giants. Others are noted in Chapter 11.

It is important to appraise not only the overall capabilities of competitors but, more importantly, their strengths and weaknesses relative to specific market segments. When Citytrust Bancorp understood the strengths of the major New York banks at large corporate accounts, it successfully shifted its thrust to smaller customers. When the owners of Häagen-Dazs ice cream found themselves outgunned in standard ice cream, they developed a super-quality product and made millions. The success of each of the personal computer manufacturers will depend largely on its ability to identify the special requirements of different market segments and to focus its offering where it can build advantages. Few show any signs of doing that; most will surely fail. Even Apple, which has unique strengths of its own, seems intent on competing directly with IBM at large corporate customers. That course is fraught with danger.

Knowing competitors' strengths can help a company shift the nature of a business in its favor. As a manufacturer of sodium borohydride, Ventron Corporation faced potential competition from Du Pont and Ethyl, basic producers of its major raw material. These larger companies had far greater capability to develop low-cost manufacturing processes. As long as sodium borohydride was sold as a bulk commodity chemical on a price basis, Ventron's future was in jeopardy. So it divided its markets into segments and developed specialized application technology for each. It incorporated the basic chemical in proprietary mixtures for different industrial uses. These special product forms together with advice on how to use them became important factors in selling to each segment. Developing a line of specialty chemicals together with the application technology for each market segment would have been too expensive for Du Pont or Ethyl to make the business attractive to them. They decided not to enter the business.

As with markets, a company can learn a great deal about its actual competitors just by being active in the same business. But it is important to look systematically at each competitor's behavior and to build a dossier on each. Does it lead or does it follow? How does it approach pricing? How strong is its marketing in each segment of the business? Its technology? Its quality? Its costs? What is its tolerance for risk? Where does it usually win and where does it lose?

Especially for potential competitors, but for actual ones as well, it is useful to tap many sources of information. Some of the same sources that yield market data, such as business journals and trade associations, can provide information on competitors. Clipping services in localities where competitors are located can provide interesting items. Reports to shareholders and documents filed with federal and local governments can be revealing. One can even get valuable information about competitors by driving by their plants or looking at their help wanted ads.

Executives usually become acquainted with their counterparts in competitive companies in meetings of business, technical, and other organizations. These encounters provide opportunities to size up their rivals. Such personal impressions should be checked against known facts about competitors' behavior. Each party may be trying to mislead the other. It is an advantage to a company to have its competitors believe its management is irrational. That makes its behavior harder to predict and its market segments less attractive for others. Some companies deliberately try to project such an image. When an executive believes that his competitors are behaving irrationally, it is more likely that he simply fails to see their reasoning or motivation.

As with markets, the key to understanding competitors is to look, to collect and to assemble data systematically, and to try to see what it means. Executives who do so are in a better position to formulate sound strategy than those who flail away blindly at competition on a day-to-day basis.

**Know Your Business Environment**

A sensible strategy cannot be formulated in a vacuum. Management needs information about the environment in which it operates if it is to identify a sound economic role for itself.

What specificallly does management need to know in order to formulate a sound strategy? This is the subject of a whole area of academic study called environmental analysis (EA). Textbooks provide long lists of items needed in EA including the size and nature of markets, economic, social, and demographic trends, government policies, competitive practices, and hundreds of other factors. Practical executives, realizing that managers cannot possibly take the time to collect, organize, record, and use all this information, typically specify an abbreviated list of key factors in their annual planning exercises. In the end, neither the long, academic list nor the shorter, practical requirement is an adequate solution to the problem.

To establish a sound strategy, executives must be aware of what is going on in the world and how it could affect their business. The critical element that makes for success or failure is frequently some circumstance no checklist of environmental factors would be likely to highlight. Each business must be viewed differently. Textbook approaches to identifying opportunities and threats are usually sterile. What is needed is executives with vision who are selective and sensitive with respect to external information:

- They must focus their fact-gathering efforts on those areas likely to be of special importance to their particular businesses.
- They must be sensitive to possible effects on their operations of other developments, whatever they may be.
- They must be able to see how changes in the business environment may open opportunities for them.

It is this kind of vision that led to Sears Roebuck's enormous success with retail stores when locations outside of city centers were made accessible by the widespread use of the automobile. It was sensitivity to the potentialities of the microprocessor that enabled Apple and Radio Shack to identify the opportunity in personal computers. It took more than routine environmental analysis to see the opportunities airline deregulation opened for newcomers such as New York Air and People's Express.

Seeing such opportunities clearly requires knowledge about what is happening in the world. The problem is that so much is going on that there is no practical way to specify which particular areas of the environment are likely to be most significant to an enterprise. There is no simple formula for becoming aware of opportunities and threats arising out of economic, technical, social, and political change. The key is to look, to think, to keep informed, and to try to see how external developments may affect the business. Continuing seriously to seek to understand how an enterprise relates to its environment helps prevent management myopia.

Some environmental trends that appear to be basic are only temporary aberrations, even though they may persist for several years. An uneconomic trend, or one leading to an absurd conclusion, will not continue indefinitely. For a time during the 70s, economic wealth was being transferred to the Arab states at a rate that would have given them all the money in the world within a decade. Such a trend could not continue. In the 80s, oil became increasingly plentiful. With a limited natural supply, that trend could not continue indefinitely either. When basing a strategy on an environmental change, management must ask itself whether it is reasonable to expect the trend to continue forever. If continuation would lead to a highly unlikely state of affairs, management must carefully examine the situation to determine what assumptions to use as a basis for its strategy.

### Know Your Company's Own Capabilities and Limitations

CEOs are successful people. They have reached their positions by accomplishing more than most of their contemporaries. They have "learned" that they can succeed through effort alone. As we have already seen, they frequently embark on ambitious projects based more on confidence in their own ability than on an objective analysis of the relative capabilities of their companies and competitors.

Even in top management, a sort of Peter Principle applies: CEOs often undertake ever more challenging enterprises until they overextend the capabilities of their companies.

The most reliable basis for appraising a company's resources is its track record. What has it done well? Where has it stumbled? Texas Instruments had failed to reach its objectives in two previous ventures in consumer products when it embarked in its disastrous foray into home computers. Bell & Howell, once a successful producer of home movie cameras, failed in each of three attempts to crack the market for still cameras. Looking at past experience might have saved each of these companies from overestimating its strengths. An analysis of its capabilities based on its past experience could have helped Beatrice Foods avoid at least some of its 50 ill-conceived acquisitions.

The differences in what a company can and cannot do well are often subtle. The fact that a company can develop and market one consumer product such as movie cameras does not necessarily mean it can succeed with another such as still cameras. We saw in Chapter 3 how Philip Morris and Coca-Cola were led to make poor investments by failing to understand what they could and could not do well. It is so easy to be misled by superficial similarities that some acquisition-minded corporations prefer to buy totally unrelated businesses. There they at least recognize that they do not know the business and leave operating decisions to unit managers. They find this approach generates better results than trying to mastermind a grand strategy based on synergy.

One way to identify the areas in which a corporation has superior capabilities is to calculate the return on capital it is already earning in each part of its business. Where a company is generating a high return, it probably has a competitive edge. For example, it once occurred to a sign painter to look at the profitability of his outdoor work relative to that of his indoor signs. Based on simple back-of-the-envelope calculations, he concluded that the indoor signs were more profitable. In light of that information, he decided to raise the price of the outdoor signs and to lower those of the others. As a result, he priced himself out of the outdoor market and boosted his indoor business. He added other products and services for the latter segment. Within several years he became one of the most successful designers of retail interiors in the country.

Few companies measure return on capital by product line or by specific customer type. Such calculations seem too difficult to be practical. Allocating overheads by product line is imprecise. So is measuring the cost to serve various customer groups. The figures must be assembled by accountants who are often compulsive about precision. But precision is not necesary. Getting a reasonable approximation can be done quickly and easily if one can induce an accountant to work with rough estimates. What is significant is big differences. Ballpark numbers can provide valuable information about what a company can or cannot do well.

Determining whether or not a corporation has the capability to compete successfully in a new area is not easy. One must identify the key determinants of success in the specific business segments involved. If one knows the market intimately or obtains the help of outsiders who do, that may not be so difficult. More challenging is the task of comparing the company's capabilities and resources with those of other suppliers. Still tougher is determining whether a company's general characteristics are suitable for the new market. Any one of a wide number of elements including operating effectiveness, approach to marketing, and attitudes toward cost, quality, customer service, risk, financial control, or other factors can prove decisive. General Motors failed in the kitchen appliance business partly because its wage scales at its Frigidaire unit reflected conditions in the automobile industry. Exxon's approach to decision making doomed its electronics business. The enormously powerful

Japanese trading companies are struggling to find ways to apply their capabilities to high-technology businesses, with little success. IBM succeeded in personal computers partly because it separated the new operation from its other activities and from their ways of doing business. Even then it was unable to succeed in the home computer segment of the market.

In appraising a company's ability, it is essential to be specific. It is not enough to recognize that a company is good at selling consumer products as Philip Morris and Coca-Cola found out. Specific capabilities such as distributing packaged products through supermarkets, building demand efficiently through TV advertising, or expertise in test marketing are what count. Selling by direct mail and through specialty boutiques require entirely different sets of skills.

The key step is to look—and to go beyond superficial generalizations. This requires effort and discipline. But the cost of determining ahead of time that a company is poorly equipped for a certain field is much lower than learning the hard way—by trying and failing.

## Segment Your Markets

As we have seen, different customers have different requirements even in the same broad market. The capabilities needed to succeed in one segment are different from those required in others. An asset in one area is a liability in others. Market segmentation is best done by grouping customers and prospects according to the key factors influencing their buying decisions. The objective is to identify those for which a company's distinctive competence affords a competitive advantage. It is a question of matching a company's capabilities with the market segments that really need them.

Segmenting markets is a little like a football coach considering the different elements of his offense: running straight ahead, running wide, passing short or passing long. He considers his strengths and weaknesses relative to those of his competitors. He then concentrates on the specific type of offense that affords his team the greatest competitive advantage against his opponent in a particular game.

In business, there are many more possibilities, so the challenge is greater. Market segmentation requires vision, creativity, and judgement. The ability to see new ways to group customers opens opportunities to find better ways to serve them. Executives should strive to develop this ability in themselves and in their employees and to encourage innovative ways to segment the market. Companies like McDonald's, Avon Products, Kmart, Polaroid, Xerox, and Sears Roebuck built enormous enterprises by defining markets in new ways. They developed the ability to serve certain customers' needs more effectively than their competitors could. Today, walk-in dental and medical clinics are doing the same thing. Gannett Corporation spotted a market for a national newspaper and started *USA Today*. It soon had the second-largest daily in the country!

During the strategy formulation procedure, the management of each operating unit should be required to segment its markets in the most useful ways it can find. More than one criterion should be explored. For example, a personal computer manufacturer might segment its market by price range, by operating system, by application, by customer type (commercial, institutional, government, professional, individual), or by other characteristics. Because it is so important, senior executives outside the operating unit should assist in this activity. Seeing how markets can best be segmented is essential to effective strategy formulation. Creative market segmentation is at the heart of nearly every successful case cited in this book as it is in business generally.

## Define Your Business

The way the business is defined will determine the extent to which a firm has opportunities to excel and to produce attractive earnings. The foundation of a strategy is the definition of which customers to serve, which of their needs to fill, and how to go about filing them. From these factors, one can deduce the characteristics of suppliers that are likely to succeed and the specific resources and capabilities to develop for competitive superiority. When management selects the market segments to address, it must already have in mind the general nature of its company and the resources and capabilities it already has in place.

As we have seen, the scope of activities a single corporation can do well is limited. The objective is to address only market segments in which the company's general nature and outstanding competence can provide decisive advantages. If a company pursues customers requiring too broad a range of resources, it will have difficulty investing enough in any one area of capability to expect to excel. The "concentrated corporation" has advantages parallel to those of the "focused factory."

Focusing too narrowly can also be risky. A company that bases a business on one very specific set of conditions is highly vulnerable to changes in the environment. For example, a European friend was in the business of selling tax-free liquor to American tourists returning home. When the U.S. government cut the amount one could bring in tax-free from one gallon to one quart, his business disappeared. Management must weigh carefully the trade-off in riskiness between being too focused and not being focused enough.

Management seeks to define its business so that its being in one market segment provides a significant advantage in another. For instance, its position in large computers gave IBM a telling advantage in personal computers for the corporate market. Management must also test segments for compatibility. Being in one segment may make it impractical to be in another. For example, selling the IBM PC through speciality computer retailers made it difficult to compete with Commodore and Atari in the market segments best reached through mass-merchandisers.

When companies fail to segment their business properly, they frequently end up trying to serve incompatible segments. The industrial supply manufacturer cited in Chapter 6 had that problem. More recently Shiseido, Japan's largest cosmetics manufacturer, has experienced similar difficulties. Traditionally Shiseido's image was upscale, top-of-the-line quality. Then they introduced lower-priced products aimed at a younger, less affluent market segment. Subsequently, they began selling through convenience stores. These moves muddied Shiseido's image. They opened the door for a competitor, Kanebo, to take an increasing share of the market using Shiseido's original cencept, focusing narrowly on the upper end of the market.

Because defining the business is so central to its nature and its success, top management must assume primary responsibility for it. But at the same time, the knowledge and insights of line executives are also necessary; this is not a task for those in an ivory tower. What this suggests is close interaction between unit managers and top management during this process, as in Japanese companies.

Divisions can be asked to make recommendations on business definitions for their operations at the same time they segment their markets. Because the general nature and capabilities of the enterprise as a whole will depend importantly on those of the divisions, it is a good idea to ask unit managers to suggest a business definition for the overall corporation as well. Even though they may lack the information needed to do that task well, it will encourage them to take into account the relation of their units' strategies to that of the corporate whole.

Recommendations of operating executives can provide top management with good ideas to use in formulating an integrated definition of the business of the overall enterprise. Extensive discussions with both line and staff are likely to be needed. The counsel of directors and professional service firms can be helpful. Ultimately the CEO must decide on the corporation's strategy, what it is to be and where it is to go.

A key issue is whether real decisions are to be made. Often, companies prepare mealymouthed, weasel-worded, catchall statements that fail to define the business in any meaningful way. The central function of strategy is to determine the capabilities in which the firm will develop the superiority and on which its competitive advantage is to be based. Unless management formulates a clear strategy, the company will attempt to be good at everything and succeed in excelling in nothing. It will be on the competitive treadmill.

**Communicate Your Decisions to the Organization**

A strategic business definition will be difficult for many managers to grasp or to accept. It runs counter to the philosophy of opportunism, yielding to immediate pressures and responding to competitive moves, which have been the fabric of most executive experience. A concentrated effort will be needed to communicate strategic decisions effectively enough that the organization will act on them.

A single pronouncement from the CEO, necessary as it may be, will have little effect. What will count more is top management behavior. Will senior executives themselves pursue the strategy seriously? Will approvals of proposals and other decisions reflect the strategy? Will the company follow the strategy in tough times as well as in good? Will compensation, recognition, and promotions depend on implementing the strategy? Will top management require that the buisness definition of each unit conform to that of the corporation? Or will the strategic thinking be emasculated by pressures for higher current earnings?

So far as straightforward communications are concerned, the key is repetition. When a new strategy is adopted, top management can arrange special meetings to discuss and to explain it. It can also provide managers with written material for future reference. Top management should then use all the means at its disposal to repeat and reinforce the message through the house organ, business review meetings, and annual and quarterly reportrs. American companies would do well to emulate the Japanese and repeat the core of the strategic thrust even in advertising, news releases, and a meaningful company slogan.

## Establish an Aggressive Resource Development Program

When the company has decided on the capabilities on which it will seek to gain a competitive advantage, it must establish a high-priority program to develop and extend its competence in these areas. Quality and quantity of new hires, the size and composition of capital and operating budgets, and the level of support in times of financial stress should all reflect the long-term importance of these programs. Consistency is necessary if a resource development program is to be productive.

Hopefully, a strategy once formulated can be followed for a period of years. If a company vacillates about its general nature, the businesses it will pursue, and the capabilities it will develop, it is unlikelly to succeed. Building competitive superiority takes commitment and persistence.

Nevertheless, management must continue to collect information, to experiment, to be able to define ever more precisely which customers it can serve best and which it cannot serve so well. Vital, progressive companies continue to probe new markets and to refine the definitions of their businesses. They discoutinue activities that do not produce an attractive return and are careful that proposed new areas genuinely promise superior rewards over the long term. Texas Instruments has probably abandoned the consumer market for a long time. McDonald's has found that it can serve the breakfast market and some foreign markets profitably. When well-managed firms have defined business segments in which they will excel, they invest aggressively in widening their competitive advantage and entrenching themselves in leadership positions.

# 9

# Planning for the Long Term

Planning is like motherhood—everyone agrees that it is good. But surprisingly few executives have taken the time to examine closely the practical role that planning should play in running a business. As a result, they frequently install procedures that fail to meet the needs of the situation. We shall suggest a more effective approach. But before discussing procedures, we shall review:

- The purpose of planning.
- The function of long-range planning.
- Dealing with uncertainty.
- The role of computer modeling.

## THE PURPOSE OF PLANNING

Planning deals with the future. Its function is to help see what to do today to achieve tomorrow's objectives and how to avoid the many pitfalls that await the unwary. It involves projecting the results of various actions under different possible circumstances. Considering potential developments and alternate ways to cope with them is the essence of planning.

One objective of planning is to determine *how* best to proceed to accomplish a complex task. For example, if one is to build a house, he will need to arrange for the proper materials and labor to be on the site at appropriate times. He will have to obtain needed permits and to provide for utilities such as electricity, water, sewerage, and telephone. The time and money required to get the job done will depend to a considerable extent on how well the needs of the project were foreseen and provided for.

This objective can often be accomplished with a single-scenario plan. Once the final design, site, and builder have been selected, the range of possible developments is narrow and can usually be taken care of in simple ways. A little extra material will be shipped to the site to take care of errors. The cost estimate may contain a contingency factor. The schedule will provide some flexibility for weather problems or other unpredictable delays. Even a single projection of what is likely to be needed will provide for a far more efficient program than simply going to the site each day to determine what to do next.

A second function planning of is to help determine *what* to do. When one first considers building a house, he does not know what kind will best suit his needs. To determine that, he must look at a variety of sizes and styles and try to foresee how each one would meet his requirements. A good planner will try to envision possible future changes he may face such as:

- Expanding the family.
- Changing income level.
- Needing an office in the home.
- Wanting live-in help.
- Seeing the children mature and leave.
- Being attracted to work in another city.

His selection of a house will depend on the implications of the entire range of reasonably possible events and how he would respond to them. He may choose a house quite different from the one he would most like to live in because, for example, he may see the likelihood of his being transferred to another city and feel the need to place resale value high on his priority list. Seeing what best to do clearly requires consideration of a variety of possible scenarios.

Companies commonly see the need for planning a long-term project and often do it well. A single-scenario plan may be quite satisfactory for laying out a specific program to get the job done. But determining *which program to pursue* to implement corporate strategy is another matter. That function requires projecting the results of different courses of action under different circumstances. For this purpose, the single-scenario plan is inadequate.

For example, a company needing more manufacturing capacity has a number of choices. It can build new facilities. It can buy existing ones and convert them to its use. It can acquire one or more companies with suitable plants. Or it can rely more on subcontractors. Each scenario merits consideration before a decision is made.

This is not to say that companies using a single, long-range projection have not considered some alternative possibilities. They usually have. But the consideration of alternatives may have been neither systematic nor thorough. Often, quantitative projections of various alternatives are not made. Moreover, many real possibilities are ignored altogether.

On one occasion, for example, the manufacturing people at Ventron, facing a onetime need to store many drums of a chemical for a long time, proposed to build a new warehouse. The financial vice president challenged the need. "Why not simply leave the drums out of doors?" he asked. He was told that in rain and snow the drums would rust. "Why not cover them with plastic sheeting?" That would reduce but not eliminate the problem. "How much would it cost to clean and repaint the drums?" Not much. The company finally decided not to build the warehouse and saved a lot of money. Without the insistence of the financial vice president that all reasonable alternatives should be considered, a misallocation of capital would surely have taken place.

Identifying alternative possibilities and selecting the best course of action, the essence of the planning function, is a basic management responsibility. The higher the management level, the more important is this activity. Unfortunately, despite the widespread interest in long-range planning, many companies still stake their futures on a single scenario of what may occur. They clearly need better planning procedures.

## FUNCTION OF LONG-RANGE PLANNING

To design effective procedures for long-range planning, it is necessary to see how its function differs from strategy formulation and budgeting. Actually, long-range planning overlaps each of the other two activities, so that they are often confused with each other. The differences may be seen by considering these activities as part of a spectrum of management responsibilities.

| Spectrum of Planning Issues | | |
|---|---|---|
| *Strategy* | *Long-Range Planning* | *Budgeting* |
| Which market segments to pursue | Resource development plans | This year's detailed capital and expense budgets |
| Which resources and capabilities to develop | Long-term operating plans | |

◄─────────────────────────────────────────────────►

| More general | | More specific |
|---|---|---|
| More permanent | | More often adjusted |

In setting its strategy, a company must determine which market segments to address and which capabilities to develop to achieve a competitive advantage there. In planning, it determines how to attack the segments it has targeted and how to build its competitive superiority. The strategy and long-range plans must shape each year's budget, which determines in detail where the company will spend its money and effort. The long-range plans must provide for both strategic and operational needs.

The fundamental differences between strategic management and operating management are reflected in differences in the long-range planning needs of each. Operations must be planned for a time period that is limited by the ability of the organization to forecast reliably. Strategic planning includes allocating money and effort to developing certain types of resources over a long period of time. Planning such expenditures several years ahead may be based only on management's general conviction that this type of investment will be needed.

These two aspects of long-range planning may apply to the same program. For example, a company may have a strategy of developing expertise in a certain area of technology. Its resource development plan will include specifying the number and types of scientific professionals, the amount and quality of lab space, and the cost implications of this buildup over a period of years. At the same time, operational plans will be needed to determine specific technical goals and the programs required to achieve them. Or a company may have a strategy to build a capability to serve a certain group of customers. Its resource development plans will provide for building a base of customer information, a sales and marketing organization, a product line, and distribution channels to serve that market segment effectively. At the same time, it will need detailed operating plans to deploy the capabilities already developed to win new customers and build sales volume in the targeted segment.

There are many situations in which decisions are crucial in both an operational and a strategic way. In an industry in which either of two technologies may win out, should a company put all its resources on one or divide its effort? Should Apple develop a computer compatible with the IBM PC or bet its future on products based on its own operating systems? How much debt should a company carry? Should it leverage itself highly to increase its return on equity, risking financial collapse if unexpected problems arise? Should an enterprise rush a product to market to be there first, risking performance problems under conditions of commercial use?

The answers to these questions require considering both operational and strategic issues. Following either side alone without considering the other is inadequate.

Plans for developing strategic resources are long-term affairs. Altering such plans can be expensive. Repeated changes can be disastrous. A research program or a campaign to build a reputation requires continuity. Hiring and firing scientists with each fluctuation in the business cycle can destroy a plan to develop outstanding technical competence. Changes in product line, marketing policy, advertising, or public relations can confuse the public with respect to what a company stands for. Plans for building the competence on which a strategy is based must be laid with the realization that there will be pressures that will make it difficult to maintain a steady course. A company that changes direction every time a new opportunity or difficulty is encountered makes little strategic progress.

Operating plans, on the other hand, must be more flexible. The company must be prepared to respond quickly to competitive moves, changes in the market, or other developments. The whole range of possibilities must be considered and plans must be made accordingly.

## DEALING WITH UNCERTAINTY

Why don't companies work harder to identify alternative scenarios and their implications? Two reasons stand out:

1. There are so many uncertainties and imponderables in connection with the future that trying to identify all of the

possibilities, to say nothing of evaluating them, seems too difficult and time-consuming.
2. Projecting the results of even one set of assumptions seems like so much work that handling a range of scenarios has seemed impractical.

Nevertheless, systematic consideration of alternatives can pay big dividends. Often, ballpark estimates point clearly toward the best approach to pursue. When more complex quantitative analyses are needed, electronic data processing is available.

What is needed in a plan depends on the degree of uncertainty involved. In long-range business planning, things are seldom predictable. They involve great uncertainty. The one thing management can be sure of is that actual events will be different from any projection it may make about conditions several years hence.

Forecasting demand is treacherous. Even economists have trouble calling the turn on the business cycle with respect to both timing and amplitude. Sales of individual products depend on fickle customers, competitive moves, and the effectiveness of one's own sales promotion program. Government regulation and deregulation can create or destroy markets overnight. So can changes in consumer tastes. Remember chlorophyll, electric skillets, hula hoops, CB radios, nuclear power, and Cabbage Patch dolls? Think of the challenge of forecasting demand five years ahead for home computers, software, large cars, walk-in medical service, or solar power devices.

Projecting sales, especially when new products are involved, suffers from another difficulty: a bias toward overoptimism. Executives, knowing that plans affect motivation and performance, often encourage subordinates to prepare plans which require reaching or stretching to achieve. Moreover, there is human tendency to confuse what one *hopes* will happen with what is *likely* to occur. Managers underestimate the time it will take to develop a new product and to get it to market. They underestimate how long it takes to get customers to change their practices and how quickly competitors respond to their initiatives. They underestimate the number of unforeseeable problems and delays that occur with any new project.

Even with established products, there is a tendency toward optimism. When the planned sales of each entrant in any industry are added together, the total exceeds what any would forecast for the market as whole.

Predicting financial conditions is just as difficult. Interest rates fluctuate. So do stock prices. One year, venture capital money is simply not available, while two years later hundreds of firms are competing for opportunities to invest in start-up companies. There are times when a company can float a stock issue at an attractive price and other times when it cannot find a market for new shares at any price. The attitudes of banks toward lending change according to their recent experience and the general economic outlook.

Foreseeing technological developments and their commercial implications is no easier. What will be the major businesses based on biotechnology or genetic engineering five or ten years from now? When will magnetohydrodynamics be economical? Will supersonic air transport ever be commercially attractive? What will be the first large-scale industrial activity in space? When will the United States adopt the metric system or standardize personal computer software?

Amid such uncertainty, executives must make commitments affecting the long-term future. If they are to avoid aimless drifting, they must act. They must formulate a strategy, adopt a plan, and move ahead. They must provide for the assets and capabilities that will be needed to achieve their objectives.

Even in a dynamic new industry, one can envision many of the issues and trends that will characterize the longer term, if he will only look. Seeing the broad outlines of a situation helps management to formulate a sound strategy.

Implementing the strategy is another matter. Management must make specific decisions currently that will determine the company's ability to compete 5 or 10 years in the future. It must commit to the new plants, establish and develop programs, hire the potential senior managers, design the information systems and organizational patterns that will shape the firm's future. It must determine how much to spend in each area. It must achieve a practical balance between fixed commitments and programs that can easily be adjusted or terminated. And it must do this in the face of great uncertainty about the details of what lies ahead.

In today's fast-changing world, there is more uncertainty than ever. Failing to recognize the implications of potential change can be fatal. Simply projecting one possible sequence of events is no longer an adequate approach to long-range planning. Management must look at alternatives. Fortunately, more effective methods for doing so are now becoming available.

## THE ROLE OF COMPUTER MODELS IN
## LONG-RANGE PLANNING

Computer models, or decision support systems (DSS) as they are called, provide effective tools for attacking the problem. They enable management easily and quickly to project possible results of a wide range of alternative actions under a variety of circumstances. They offer insights as to which expenditures are most critical, with respect both to building a better future and to avoiding problems.

DSS software has long been available for larger computers. However, using them—integrating them into a company's pattern of top management decision making—has proven difficult. DSS software for mainframe computers has been cumbersome to install. Companies have found it can take a year or more to get such a system up and running. Computer experts and senior executives rarely think alike. Communications between them is sometimes so difficult that the system is ineffective. As a result, management has tended to use them primarily as sophisticated tools for analyzing specific major investments rather than as a way to develop a broader vision of the overall corporate financial situation or of the implications of alternative plans.

Convenient software has now been developed to facilitate modeling on personal computers. Because they can be made available on short notice and are so easy to operate, personal computers make DSS much more practical for use by top management. This development promises to revolutionize the way many decisions are made in the executive suite and in the board room.

Creating a financial model of a company is not difficult. Management makes whatever assumptions it wishes about growth, profitability, expenditure patterns, financial ratios, and how each factor is likely to affect results. These assumptions are plugged into the computer. Then management can vary the assumptions in whatever way it finds useful. Within seconds, the computer projects the future based on these assumptions for as many years as is useful. One can quickly see which combinations of decisions and circumstances are promising or are dangerous. Similarly, one learns which assumptions are critical and therefore should be examined more closely. Making the assumptions explicit, as modeling requires, stimulates management consideration of questions that might otherwise remain unasked.

In this book, we have recommended doing strategy formulation and long-range planning separately and at different times. But we must not forget that they are but two aspects of the task of management. Many areas involve both long-range planning and strategy. Computer modeling can provide insights relevant to both.

A model can, for example, indicate the effect of increased research spending on earnings in future years under various assumptions. With such information at hand, management is in a better position to decide how much to commit to more or less permanent R&D staff and facilities, how much to allocate to research projects done by outside labs that can be terminated on short notice, and how much to channel elsewhere.

During the annual planning exercise, management must keep strategic issues in mind. How much spending on research in a given area is likely to be required to provide a meaningful competitive edge? To what extent are unpredictable opportunities likely to be identified later as a result of developing and introducing a new product line? Answers to questions such as these sometimes reveal that a company's basic strategy is unsound and that another course is likely to be much better.

Companies have begun using computer simulation and qualitative judgment together with good results. For example, a $400 million service firm consisted of two principle operating groups. The older one, which represented the bulk of the business, showed good earnings and was seen to have good growth opportunities. The newer group was in an emerging business with potentially explosive growth possibilities. Management was allocating virtually all of its discretionary spending to expanding the new area.

Under the direction of the financial vice president, a simple computer model was developed. Results over the next five years were projected using different assumptions about the allocation of capital between the two groups under various assumptions. Surprisingly, even with what appeared to be optimistic assumptions about the newer business, pouring more money into it did not promise better results. Because it was more capital-intensive, return on investment was not higher. Moreover, it was in a more uncertain market with much greater risks. On the other hand, it could possibly lead to more growth opportunity in the longer term.

Management decided to shift its capital allocation and to invest more in the older part of the business. In the event, the newer group ran into unexpected trouble and suffered heavy losses. One source of the problem was the difficulty the organization had in managing rapid growth. In hindsight, it appeared that if the company had continued to pour all its available funds into the smaller division, it would have made the problem even worse.

A New York Stock Exchange corporation used a computer model to project the impact of various possible dividend policies on the price of its shares at different times. Under the financial constraints faced by the company, it was clear that increasing cash dividends would either limit the corporate growth rate or increase its cost of capital. The influences of these effects along with different assumptions about how the market responds to cash dividends were fed into the model. The exercise made it clear that in this situation, higher cash dividends would reduce the value of the shares, except possibly in the very short run.

Another company of similar size used a more sophisticated model, still on a personal computer, to understand better the implications of various capital allocations among 15 operating divisions. Many alternative scenarios were considered. The possibilities for hypothetical acquisitions were also considered. The result contributed to a better understanding about how different capital allocation patterns might affect long-term performance.

## PROCEDURES FOR LONG-RANGE PLANNING

Long-range planning is a bridge between strategy and operations. It provides insights about the long-term effects of current expenditures. Such insights are needed to guide the preparation of annual capital and operating budgets. Key elements of long-range planning and factors commonly leading to failure are shown in the box on page 126.

Long-range planning should be done annually before preparing the annual budget. Adequate time must be allowed for the planning process, for budgeting, and for revising the budget if that becomes necessary. The entire exercise could take up to five months: about two months for long-range planning, about two months for budgeting, and one month "cushion" at the end in case revision is necessary. Companies skilled in annual planning procedures can often do the job in considerably less time. But the schedule should provide for presenting annual plans to the board about a month before the end of the fiscal year. An effective long-range planning sequence is discussed below.

---

### KEY ELEMENTS OF LONG-RANGE PLANNING

1. Envision a range of possible future scenarios with respect to market trends, competitive moves, business climate, and company programs. Cover the time span needed to determine the best current course of action.
2. Consider how the company would respond to various developments. Project pro forma financial statements for the major alternative possibilities.
3. Determine a current course of action taking into account the potential risks and costs of a change in direction being necessitated by unexpected events.
4. Establish checkpoints and criteria for deciding whether and how to modify the program or action.

### FACTORS COMMONLY LEADING TO INADEQUATE LONG-RANGE PLANNING

1. Misunderstanding the basic function of planning.
2. Preoccupation with short-term pressures and problems.
3. Skepticism about and discomfort with expending serious effort trying to determine how best to prepare for a highly uncertain future.
4. Failure to recognize the importance of dealing with the broad range of reasonably possible developments: Putting too much emphasis on what to do under a single set of questionable assumptions.

---

### Step 1: Fix the Period of Time to Be Covered

The purpose of a plan is to help guide current decisions. If long-range plans are prepared annually, the only decisions affected by the plan are those to be made in the 12 months following its preparation. Subsequent decisions will be guided by revised plans. Thus the planning period should be only long enough to include possibilities that will affect decisions to be made in the current year.

The full effects of some decisions such as building new facilities, entering new markets, or even changing price policies or the financial structure may not manifest themselves for several years. A company should not shrink from projecting situations more than five years in the future. Even though events at that time may be quite impossible to forecast accurately, alternative long-term projections can still help evaluate various possible current decisions.

Inevitably, it will be possible and necessary to plan some aspects of a business much further into the future than others. If a company chooses five years as the term for the corporate plan, it may still find it desirable to plan further ahead in particular areas such as facilities, executive manpower, or refunding of debt. In other areas such as product development specific plans for four or five years ahead may be all but meaningless. Once can still make reasonable estimates of how spending may relate to other dimensions of the company several years out without knowing what the specifics may be. The key to the planning period is what is needed to determine how best to manage this year, not the clarity with which one can see the future in one aspect of the business or another.

The appropriate operational planning period varies widely from one industry to another. Plans for companies manufacturing airframes or refining oil may appropriately extend over 10 years or even more. In many areas in the electronics industry, it is almost impossible to plan a product development activity more than a year or two in advance. In the ladies' garment industry, product planning may be limited to a period of weeks. However, even there long-range planning can be extremely helpful. In any case, management should be guided by what is appropriate for its particular situation, not by what others may be doing.

### Step 2: Identify Alternative External Scenarios

Long-range planning begins with assembling information about the business environment. The company should have been collecting relevant data throughout the year. The corporate office, perhaps with help from a bank or other outside source, should develop alternative scenarios of external economic conditions. The company's research staff can provide opinions, perhaps with the help of outside consultants, about possible technical developments. The marketing department can help forecast changes in customer requirements and competitive moves. Manufacturing management can try to foresee how the development of new technology, methods, equipment, or systems may affect production operations.

Top management assembles this information and exercises its own judgment in determining what external developments the company must be prepared to handle. One of its basic responsibilities is continually to scan the horizon for important opportunities and risks that the company must be ready to meet. The annual planning exercise simply represents an occasion for doing this job more systematically and thoroughly than can be achieved on an informal basis.

### Step 3: Prepare a Computerized Financial Model of the Company

A personal computer is adequate for any but the largest, most complex situation. Usually it is best to avoid a lot of excessive detail; the objective is to see the big picture. It is important that the model be easy for top management to understand and to use. A remote mainframe computer requiring a crew of technicians to operate and a year to program may be much less useful than a PC which is immediately available. The modeling is intended to sharpen management vision of its situation: It is important to be able to explore easily whatever alternatives appear to be most interesting and important.

The model should be able to generate summary earnings statements, balance sheets, and statements of sources and applications of funds over the planning period. Convenient software for this task is readily available.

### Step 4: Explore the Effects of Alternative Possibilities

Using the computer model, management should explore the financial effects of various decisions under different assumptions about the business environment. It should observe the sensitivity of the system to different patterns of expenditure and of capital investment under different assumptions about the effects of each. It should test the sensitivity of the system to different financial possibilities such as different debt:equity ratios, interest rates, stock prices, dividend policies, or reacquisition of company securities.

In addition to examining financial effects of various alternatives, management must also consider other aspects of future possibilities. It must think about how current decisions may affect the adequacy of its human resources for achieving future objectives. It must think about the needs and availability of physical facilities over a period of years.

Top management must also take into consideration possible qualitative results of alternative courses of action. Effects on morale, company reputation, ability to attract investment or new talent, community relations, and other areas can be crucial to a decision. Where such factors can be incorporated into the financial model, that may prove useful. What is essential is that top management not let the power of the computer to deal with quantitative issues lead it to neglect the qualitative side of things.

### Step 5: Determine the Relative Merits of Alternative Budgets

The annual budget is what is used to control expenditures. Unless exceptions are made, operating decisions must conform to it. The primary purpose of the long-range plan is to help evaluate the implications of alternative scenarios for the next year's annual budget. A limited number of computer projections covering the range of reasonably possible alternatives should be selected for study in greater depth. The effects of different budgets under various assumptions should be estimated. For example if Budget A is established and market conditions are much better or much worse than the base assumption, what would be the probable result over the short and long run? At what rate would spending be increased or decreased from budgeted levels? What would be the ultimate cost of being too optimistic and establishing excessive expenditure levels? What would be the cost of holding expenses too low and perhaps losing sales and market share? How would results compare if instead Budget B were adopted?

### Step 6: Establish a Tentative Summary Budget or Variable Budgets

This step ends the long-range planning process. As detailed budgeting proceeds, it may become necessary to modify the original model. The long-range planning exercise should again be used as a guide should modification be required. Ultimately, management must decide on the spending pattern for the company for the budget period.

### Step 7: Revise Spending Plans during the Year As Required by Events

Reality rarely has the civility to conform to a budget. The long-range planning model can continue to be useful during the year to interpret longer-term effects of variances in current performance and to help determine which adjustments should be made in spending. It can also be useful for evaluating opportunities or problems that were not foreseen in the budget.

A procedure as outlined above gets directly at the purpose of long-range planning: to help select the best program of current spending from among an infinity of possibilities. It helps management see the risks and possibilities before the company and how best to deal with them. It helps avoid the most serious of all business problems—running out of money. Effective long-range planning also helps executives develop vision.

# 10

# Establishing Financial Policies

Financial policies are a vital part of a company's game plan. In defining a firm's business, management must give careful consideration to its financial capabilities relative to the needs of the situation. This should be an integral part of corporate strategy.

Finance is also a basic component of a sound long-range plan. Businesses must have money in order to operate. They need funds to build the capabilities on which future profits will depend. They must provide for enough financial flexibility to withstand periods of adversity and to seize new opportunities that come along. Eventually, they must make cash payments to their investors. At the same time, they must control the cost of the capital they use. The soundness of a company's financial policies and plans will determine not just how successful it may be but whether it survives at all.

For example, a small company near Boston developed a new medical diagnostic instrument. It was familiar with the market and knew it was large. When it exhibited a prototype of its new product, it received an enthusiastic response from potential users. Management knew it had a winner!

Supported by short-term bank borrowing, it expanded its plant. It hired a sales force. It was soon inundated with orders. It quickly scaled up production. The sweet smell of success was exhilarating—until the company ran out of money. Management had failed to consider how much cash would be needed to expand so rapidly. Alarmed by the deteriorating financial ratios and disturbed by the lack of financial planning, the bank refused to renew the loan. The company had to suspend operations until new money and new management could be brought in.

Small companies are not the only ones that run out of money. Penn Central, W. T. Grant, Itel, Wickes, and Baldwin-United are only a few of the corporate giants that have had to declare bankruptcy because they lacked the funds to continue to operate. Others such as Lockheed, Chrysler, and Continental Illinois were saved from collapse only by aid from the federal government.

These disasters were not inevitable. They occurred because the managements failed in financial planning. In the case of the medical equipment company, there were virtually no financial plans at all; management simply plunged ahead based on its confidence in its product. The larger companies no doubt had prepared projections of their needs and sources for funds. But because their plans were flawed they were unable to meet their financial requirements.

Too often, financial planning becomes a complex web of accounting procedures that obscure rather than elucidate the fundamental situation. To manage its financial affairs wisely, management must have a clear overview of the major elements of its position.

The principal cash flows occasioned by corporate activity are present in Chart 10–1 on page 133. For the shareholders and lending institutions, a corporation is an investment vehicle. It moves investors' funds to current operations, to building capabilities to create future values, and perhaps to other investments. When operations generate more money than the corporation can invest advantageously, it can move cash back in the investors.

Looking at this simplified financial model of an enterprise raises obvious questions about some common practices. Why pay cash dividends if there are opportunities to reinvest all of a firm's cash in operations promising a superior return? Does reinvesting money in the company help the shareholders if they have better investment opportunities for their funds elsewhere? Since the investors can direct their cash to any number of companies, how does diversification of a single enterprise serve their interests? Does a corporation serve any valid economic function when it simply channels money to other companies? Addressing fundamental questions such as these can help executives develop the kind of vision needed to deal rationally with financial management rather than to rely on convention or on the advice of biased outsiders.

Another basic approach to seeing financial questions in perspective is to scan the business horizon for alternative possibilities and determine their financial implications. Using computer modeling as described in Chapter 9 is an excellent means for developing financial vision. It can result in a far more effective game plan than

**CHART 10–1**  Typical Corporate Cash Flows

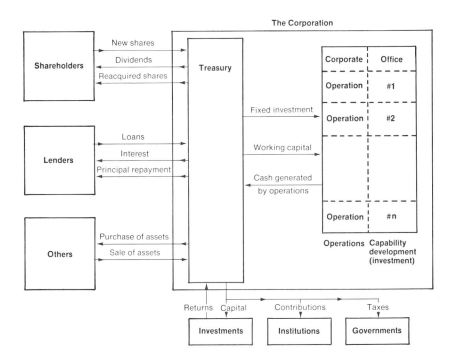

basing strategies on intuition and judgment alone, using a single "most likely" scenario.

Financial planning has three major objectives:

1.  Provide needed funds at minimum cost.
2.  Guide investment activities.
3.  Determine when and how to channel cash to stockholders.

In many situations, two or more objectives are in conflict and management faces the task of striking an appropriate compromise.

To executives whose primary experience has been in other areas, finance often seems like an arcane world in which wizardry is needed for success. Actually, it is straightforward, although there is plenty of room for imaginative techniques just as in any other field. Basic elements of financial planning and common causes of financial problems are listed in the box on page 134. These items are not so mysterious. An executive with the vision to see the big picture and with the determination to explore the results of alternative actions under a range of circumstances should have little difficulty making sound financial decisions.

---

### ELEMENTS OF FINANCIAL PLANNING

1. Determine the need for operating capital under various assumptions.
2. Evaluate the financial implications of various investment opportunities and capital allocation patterns.
3. Estimate the tangible and intangible costs of various sources of capital both external and internal.
4. Maintain flexibility needed to handle unforeseen problems and opportunities.
5. Weigh the relative value to owners of:
   reinvesting in the business;
   building liquidity;
   disbursing cash to stockholders;
6. Determine when to:
   pay cash dividends;
   repurchase company shares;
   transfer other assets to shareholders.
7. Develop an integrated program to provide funds for current operations and for investment consistent with interests of the shareholders.

### COMMON CAUSES OF FINANCIAL PROBLEMS

1. Inability to operate profitably.
2. Failure to foresee the need for or to control working capital.
3. Misallocation of capital.
4. Inadequate financial flexibility.
5. Looking to conventional wisdom rather than the needs of the specific situation as a guide to financial policies.

---

## FUNDS FOR OPERATIONS

### Forecasting Needs

Any company must have funds for operations. The managers of the medical equipment company cited above did not understand the effects of rapid growth on working capital requirements. They were not aware of the danger of trying to support long-term expansion with short-term borrowing. Even so, they might have spotted the trouble they were getting into *if they had only looked*. The most rudimentary financial plan would have shown that they lacked the funds to support the rapid scaleup of operations they attempted. If they had looked ahead, they might also have recognized the danger in using short-term borrowing to support long-term financial needs.

Financial crises reflect failure to consider possible adverse developments and their implications. Sometimes the very complexity and sophistication of financial projections of larger firms lead executives to put too much faith in them. They lose sight of the weakness of the underlying assumptions.

The basic approach to projecting cash needs is straightforward. Production requires investment in labor, materials, and overhead expenses before sales are made. The seller normally must wait for a period of time before he collects his money. Experience is usually a reliable guide to the timing of these various elements. It is not difficult to develop cash forecasts at various levels of activity under different assumptions. If sales increase, there will be a need for more working capital. During the initial period of greater production, before the level of collections rises, the need for cash can increase sharply, as the medical instruments company found out. Changes in margins, product mix, asset turnover or other factors will also affect cash flows, sometimes drastically.

Providing for unexpected events is more difficult. For example, a long strike, a sharp rise in interests rates, and a severe recession contributed to International Harvester's problems. No one could have predicted those events with confidence. The company's experience provided little help. Yet in every situation, there is the potential for such unexpected difficulties. Management must consider the likelihood and impact of a range of possibilities as it contemplates whether to take a strike, to build a new plant, or to make an acquisition.

Cash planning requires reviewing alternative sources of funds as well as potential needs. A company in good condition can usually get the cash it needs without problems. In a crisis, potential sources of cash quickly dry up. But a company may still have a variety of alternatives. Payables can be stretched out. Collections can be accelerated. Inventories can be shrunk. Assets that are not needed—including whole divisions—can be liquidated. Even essential assets such as plants and equipment can be sold and leased back. Sometimes intangibles such as patents, know-how, or exclusive rights of one sort or another can be converted to cash. Top management must be aware of its potential sources of funds under various conditions as it faces decisions about committing additional investment.

## RAISING CAPITAL

From time to time, companies must raise additional capital. This is a basic activity, affecting corporate control, value, and financial flexibility. Approaching the subject narrowly, focusing on short-term cost effects, is hazardous. Wise decisions depend on having the vision to see a company's capital structure broadly, considering its importance in an uncertain future.

Many different sources of capital are available. A company may sell stock or bonds either to the public or to private investors. It may borrow from banks on either a short-term basis or for a period of several years. Government entities offer favorable financing arrangements as inducements to build new plants or otherwise create employment opportunities. Companies may obtain buildings, equipment, or vehicles by leasing them. It can sell assets it already owns and lease them back. Sometimes companies can acquire capital advantageously from suppliers or customers.

Debt is usually a cheaper source of capital than equity as Exhibit 10–1 illustrates. With debt, however, a company acquires a fixed-interest obligation. Profits before debt service requirements fluctuate. Because payments to creditors are fixed, debt increases the volatility of net earnings. How this happens is illustrated in Exhibit 10–2. The range of net earnings increases from 3:1 to 6:1 because of borrowing. Because of this effect, debt is often called leverage.

When a company incurs long-term debt, it must usually accept convenants in the loan agreement to maintain prescribed financial ratios and to limit specified types of cash outflows under certain conditions. In periods of economic adversity, a company with a heavy debt burden may lack both the money and the ability to raise capital to take advantage of attractive business opportunities. Thus heavy use of debt financing reduces a company's financial flexibility and increases the risk of insolvency.

The optimum way to finance an enterprise depends on the business situation. When stable earnings can be predicted with confidence, as was traditionally the case with electric utilities, a company can safely use a great deal of debt. But when a company undertakes less predictable projects such as constructing a nuclear power plant, a heavy debt load can turn out to be dangerous. Management must be alert to changes in its basic situation as it formulates its financial

---

**EXHIBIT 10–1**   Relative Cost Of Equity Versus Debt in Raising Capital
                   Assumptions

---

ASSUMPTIONS

Company A has 1 million shares issued and outstanding. Its net worth is $20 million ($20 per share). Earnings are $2 million ($2 per share). It has an opportunity to invest $10 million on which it will earn $3.2 million annually before income tax. Its net income tax rate, considering state and federal duties, is 50 percent.

Case A.  Sell 625 thousand shares at $16 (8 times earnings).
Case B.  Sell 400 thousand shares at $25 (12½ times earnings).
Case C.  Borrow $10 million at 12 percent.
Case D.  Borrow $10 million at 16 percent

COST OF FINANCING

| Case | A | B | C | D |
|---|---|---|---|---|
| Original pretax earnings | $4,000,000 | $4,000,000 | $4,000,000 | $4,000,000 |
| Original net earnings | $2,000,000 | $2,000,000 | $2,000,000 | $2,000,000 |
| Original earnings per share | $2 | $2 | $2 | $2 |
| Pretax earnings after investment | $7,200,000 | $7,200,000 | $7,200,000 | $7,200,000 |
| Less additional interest cost | — | — | $1,200,000 | $1,600,000 |
| Net pretax earnings | $7,200,000 | $7,200,000 | $6,000,000 | $5,600,000 |
| Net earnings after 50 percent income tax | $3,600,000 | $3,600,000 | $3,000,000 | $2,800,000 |
| Number of shares outstanding | 1,625,000 | 1,400,000 | 1,000,000 | 1,000,000 |
| Earnings per share | $2.22 | $2.57 | $3.00 | $2.80 |

---

plans. Continuing traditional financing patterns while entering unfamiliar territory has led to financial crisis at a number of electric utility companies.

Conversely, whether to make an investment can depend on the nature of financing available to make it possible. For example, on one occasion when Ventron Corporation was deeply in debt, it had an opportunity to make an attractive acquisition for cash. Banks were willing to lend the money on a short-term basis. But management, after considering the possibility and consequeces of unfavorable developments, decided it would be too risky simply to borrow the money and proceed.

The company's investment bankers indicated that it was likely that Ventron could sell new shares to the public at an attractive price after the acquisition had taken place. The company's bank, after being apprised of the situation, guaranteed to convert the

---

**EXHIBIT 10–2**  Effect of Debt on Earnings Volatility

---

### ASSUMPTIONS

- Company B has 1 million shares outstanding and no debt.
- Company C has 500 thousand shares outstanding and $10 million in debt at 12 percent.
- Both companies' earnings fluctuate between $2 million and $6 million depending on economic conditions.

### EARNINGS CALCULATIONS

| Year | 1 | 2 | 3 |
|---|---|---|---|
| Earnings before tax and interest (both companies) | $4,000,000 | $6,000,000 | $2,000,000 |
| Interest cost | | | |
| Company B (no debt) | 0 | 0 | 0 |
| Company C (leveraged) | $1,200,000 | $1,200,000 | $1,200,000 |
| Net pretax earnings | | | |
| Company B (no Debt) | $4,000,000 | $6,000,000 | $2,000,000 |
| Company C (leveraged) | $2,800,000 | $4,800,000 | $ 800,000 |
| Earnings after 50 percent income tax | | | |
| Company B (no debt) | $2,000,000 | $3,000,000 | $1,000,000 |
| Company C (leveraged) | $1,400,000 | $2,400,000 | $ 400,000 |
| Earnings per share | | | |
| Company B (no debt) | $2 | $3 | $1 |
| Company C (leveraged) | $2.80 | $4.80 | $.80 |
| Ratio of earnings to Year 3 | | | |
| Company B (no debt) | 2:1 | 3:1 | 1:1 |
| Company C (leveraged) | 3.5:1 | 6:1 | 1:1 |

---

short-term debt to a longer-term loan if the proposed underwriting fell through. In light of these factors, Ventron made the acquisition. Shortly thereafter, it was able to sell enough new equity to pay off all of its debt.

Because debt usually seems cheaper than equity, companies are continually tempted to use too much of it. From time to time, an entrepreneur will build a corporate empire based primarily on borrowing. While things are going well, he is considered a financial wizard. But when the enterprise becomes too complex to manage or when the economy turns down, such structures often collapse.

Sound financing decisions require the experience and vision to consider their implications under a broad range of circumstances.

The cost of equity financing, both absolutely and relative to debt, depends on the price of a company's shares. To the extent that a company can enhance the price of its stock, it can reduce its cost of capital and increase the value of its owners' investment. The most important things management can do to make its company's shares attractive to investors are:

1. Earn a superior return on capital already invested in the company.
2. Demonstrate an ability to find and exploit additional attractive investment opportunities.

When management does well in these two ways, a company's shares are normally given a high value in the market.

Companies often look for short-cuts to enhancing the price of their shares. They produce elaborate financial reports, "manage" earnings to give the appearance of steady growth, build a record of regular dividend increases, split the stock frequently, advertise in the financial or even in the general press, hire financial PR counsel, and court the financial community however they can.

How effective are such efforts? Usually, not very. Some analysts react negatively to elaborate programs to promote a company's shares. They may become suspicious of a company whose executives spend so much time touting their stock. Carried to extremes, such activities are counterproductive. When I joined Bell & Howell, it seemed that half of the effort of the officer group was directed toward financial PR rather than to the operations that ultimately determine the value of its stock. For more than two decades afterwards, its shares sold for less than the price of the options I received when I joined the company.

In another situation, a major investor in a company stopped in to see how the firm was doing. When he left, he immediately sold his entire investment. His reason was that while he was there, his conversation with the president had been interrupted several times by the company's investment bankers reporting on the price of the firm's shares. The investor felt that the president's attention was oriented toward the price of the shares rather than on managing the business. It turned out that his decision to sell was a good one.

Unfortunately, many sources of outside counsel available to a CEO with limited financial experience must be considered suspect.

Some advisors base their recommendations largely on conventional wisdom, which may not stand up to close scrutiny. Some notions about financial policy stem from what stockbrokers find useful for selling shares to naive investors. Investment bankers, lawyers, accountants, and other service firms to which executives naturally turn for advice are often in a conflict of interest situation. The size of their fees often depends on which course of action a company takes.

In finance as in other areas, wise decisions depend on managerial vision. Basing decisions on narrow, short-term effects, on old saws, or on the advice of organizations that have their own interest to consider can lead to actions that may debilitate a company for years or even destroy it. Especially when deciding about financing, management needs the vision to recognize how unpredictable the future is and act accordingly.

## INVESTING FOR THE LONG TERM

Investment opportunities come naturally to operating companies. Potential customers seek them out. Their marketing organizations identify emerging needs for new products and services. Their manufacturing and engineering people have ideas about new equipment and facilities to improve efficiency. One of the elements of value in any company is the potential represented by the investment opportunities that are likely to come its way. One of management's major responsibilities is to recognize, to evaluate, and to exploit these opportunities.

Many managers fail to recognize that their responsibility for finding and evaluating investment opportunities is quite different from their operating responsibilities. They complain about being required to prepare detailed analyses justifying proposed capital investments. "It's silly," they say. "The board requires all this documentation before approving a $10 million capital expenditure while they exercise almost no supervision over the $20 million I spend each year in operations. The annual depreciation represented by this investment will represent only a small percentage of our total cost of goods sold. A dollar spent is a dollar spent. The board should give equal attention to money spent regardless of whether it is a capital investment or not."

Such comments reflect management myopia. The speakers do not understand the difference between the effects of fixed investments and current expenditures. They do not see the pervasive, long-term influence of a company's fixed assets on its profitability. They overlook the difference in risk between continuing existing profitable operations and expansion into new activities. They ignore the fact that the company has much more freedom of choice in decisions about committing to new operations. Their thinking is fixed on current operations. They may not understand the fundamental importance of building superior capabilities to serve carefully defined market segments.

As Chart 10–1 suggests, capital investment decisions are different from normal expenditures to support current operations. So are expenditures to build capabilities aimed at uncertain payoffs at some time in the future. These long-term investments will affect the fundamental nature of the enterprise, the definition of its business, and its success over an extended period. Seeing the full range of implications of a proposed investment is a greater challenge than evaluating the need for labor or raw materials. It is entirely appropriate for investment decisions to be approached differently, to involve greater consideration by higher levels of management.

### Evaluating Investments

Evaluating investment opportunities presents management with a challenging problem. Different projects have different purposes, different life expectancies, different patterns of cash generation, and different degrees of risk. Comparing such dissimilar possibilities can be difficult, even after assumptions have been made about the likely financial effects of each.

In order to facilitate the evaluation of alternative opportunities, companies often use techniques such as net present value (NPV) or internal rate of return (IRR) based on the concept of discounted cash flow (DCF). By discounting future cash flows, one computes their present value, making it possible to compare directly projects of dissimilar financial characteristics.

Unfortunately, these techniques, elegant as they are, can be misleading. In an article entitled "Managing Our Way to Economic Decline," William J. Abernathy and Robert H. Hayes (*Harvard Business Review*, July–August 1980) attribute America's failure to invest adequately in the future to the widespread use of DCF as the major determinant of investment decisions. In a subsequent article, "Managing as if Tomorrow Mattered," (*Harvard Business Review*, May–June 1982), Robert Hayes and David Garvin present specific sources of the difficulties involved in using DCF.

One weakness of methods based on DCF is that they do not take into account unforeseeable new opportunities that may result from having made a given investment. It is usually impossible to predict the specific nature of the opportunities that may arise much less to describe their financial characteristics. But in many cases, the long-term financial impact of opportunities growing out of a project are more important than profit directly resulting from the project itself. Wise evaluation of investment proposals requires vision to determine their value as basic capabilities and as potential sources of additional attractive opportunities, as well as their potential direct effects on earnings. Quantitative evaluation techniques can sometimes provide insights into the relative merits of similar projects, but they should be used with caution.

## Expanding Current Operations

In seeking investment opportunities, managers usually first consider expanding their existing operations. Often their thinking is affected by the apparent short-term profit impact of incremental sales. But long-term effects must be carefully considered too. Serious strategic errors can result from making investments based on short-term operational thinking alone.

For example, a diversified corporation pursued an acquisition prospect in the same industry as the firm's weakest division. Management forecast large immediate savings through consolidation. The combined company would require only one general manager, one plant, one sales force, one engineering group, and one accounting department. The product lines would be consolidated into a smaller number of items that could be produced more efficiently.

Because of these savings, the acquisition was projected to be highly profitable. Assuming it would retain only 80 percent of the volume of the acquired operation, management forecast an attractive return on the money to be invested.

Looking at the situation from a broader perspective showed a different picture. Other units of the corporation had been exceeding the corporate standard of 35 percent pretax return on capital. This division had been forecasting only 20 percent. Actually, the unit had barely broken even in recent years due to adverse market conditions, so that even the 20 percent forecast was questionable. And the company it proposed to acquire had been losing money!

The glowing financial projections resulted from the basic assumption that the combined operations would have much lower expenses per unit than they had had separately. Management recognized that overhead expenses in larger companies are often higher relative to sales than in smaller firms. In fact, it believed that even in this industry, a much larger company would probably find it impossible to keep unit overheads as low as the division was already achieving. Yet it was so entranced by the possibilities of immedite savings that it ignored the fact that by enlarging its operations, it too would probably end up with higher overhead expenses as a percent of sales.

Division management was recommending increasing investment in an industry in which it had been unable to earn satisfactory return in the past. It offered no fundamental reason for expecting a larger entity to achieve better results in the long run. It lost sight of the long-term implications of its proposal. It suffered from management myopia.

General managers nearly always believe that they can expand sales without increasing overhead. In the short term they are correct. If they ship more today, this week, this month, or this quarter, overhead expenses may not rise. But as an enterprise becomes larger and more complex, overhead expenses rise more rapidly than sales. Expanding an operation on the assumption that overheads will not rise as much as sales volume is naive.

The Boston Consulting Group has accumulated convincing evidence that overhead expenses per unit of output is higher in larger firms. Among seven dairy firms studied, those with more delivery routes had higher general and administrative costs as a percentage of sales. Among 14 custom software houses, sales per employee varied inversely with the size of the firm. Similarly, among seven advertising agencies, billings per employee tended to decline as the number of people in each office increased. The BCG data confirms the common knowledge that large corporations have higher overhead rates than smaller ones.

In planning expansion, executives with vision will recognize the tendency for overhead to rise with size. They will be skeptical of the short-range view that growth alone will reduce unit overheads. It is true that economies of scale in production, product engineering, advertising, or elsewhere can provide advantages in certain circumstances. But proposals based on the assumption that unit sales, general, and administrative costs will be lower in the long run simply because an operation is larger require careful scrutiny.

When companies add products to the line or diversify, the tendency of unit overhead costs to rise is even more pronounced. BCG data for hand tool producers, lift truck manufacturers, and chemical processing units all show overhead per unit rising with the number of different products involved. The added overhead burden resulting from increased complexity of operations must be recognized if financial plans are to be a useful guide to management decisions.

Investing in a weak division is usually a mistake. Management must determine the basic cause of poor results and consider whether it can be corrected. If the company has no reasonable opportunity to develop a fundamental competitive advantage in the area, it will do better to reduce rather than to increase its investment in that field. If, on the other hand, the difficulty is simply in managerial effectiveness, the first order of business is to correct the management problem, not to add to it by expanding.

## Investing in New Fields

When a company has difficulty finding investment opportunities in its own fields, it looks elsewhere. Entering new fields offers excitement, prestige, and potential financial rewards to senior executives. In recent years, the concept of portfolio management and the success of some conglomerates have provided a convenient rationale for diversification.

Cyclicality represents a financial problem management must deal with. Adding a countercyclical business may tend to level the company's reported earnings, but it represents another set of problems for management. Finding countercyclical businesses is difficult, as TWA learned the hard way. Even when one does, having one unit booming while another is suffering may prove to be more distracting than helpful. Unless personnel and assets can be shifted back and forth between the divisions, the economic value of such a combination is more apparent than real.

Executives with vision focus on long-term return on capital as their primary criterion in investing. When projecting results, they examine basic underlying strategic factors that will be the primary determinants of profitability over the long run. The goal of achieving some sort of balance in an investment portfolio must not be allowed to obscure a company's fundamental role as a creator of economic value.

Most corporations have some operations that earn much more than others. As the sign company cited in Chapter 8 demonstrated, the return on investment a company is already generating in its various activities can provide valuable insights for capital allocation decisions. Most companies have a few operations, products, or customer groups that contribute the bulk of their earnings. These represent the activities for which a company's unique capabilities are best suited. They usually provide the best opportunity for additional investments.

Similarly, many firms have funds invested in losing activities. For example, executives of a savings bank became curious about the relative cost of deposits from various types of customers. One group was largely blue-collar workers. They kept an average balance of about $100 in the bank, primarily to have the opportunity to cash their weekly pay-checks there. The total cost to the bank per dollar of these deposits was enormous because activity was so high and the number of dollars so low.

The average account of another group of depositors exceeded $10,000. Typically, the activity of these accounts was low, which meant that they cost little to maintain. A rough analysis revealed that the cost per deposit dollar of the former group was more than 50 times that of the latter! Clearly, investing in building local branches to cater to the needs of smaller depositors did not contribute to the profitability of the bank.

Managers with vision will identify such situations and change them. Sometimes costs can be reduced or prices raised. In other cases, shrinking or eliminating an activity can permit major overhead reductions and add to earnings. The stock in trade of many successful consulting firms includes the ability simply to identify losing operations and to show clients how to get rid of them. I have served as a director of several companies that greatly added to their value by performing radicl surgery on themselves. I described four of these case histories in "Cutting Corporations Down To Size" (*Harvard Business Review*, September–October 1984). One, Aerovox/AVX, was cited in Chapter 3.

Two of the others were Tech/Ops and Helix. Tech/Ops shares sold for under $4 when its sales exceeded $100 million. After it narrowed its scope and reduced sales to under $30 million, its share price topped $50! Helix Technology Corporation got into trouble by diversifying, and its stock price fell to about $2. Four years later, when it had shed most of its operations and concentrated on its core business, the stock sold above $35.

The shares of many companies sell for less than the value of their component parts. Corporate raiders take advantage of such situations, buying control and dismembering the business to realize its intrinsic worth. Managers with vision will recognize when combining several businesses detracts from their value and will find ways to redeploy assets more favorably. If they do not, they may find others doing it for them!

Building on demonstrated strength is a sound approach to investment. Even in mature industries, companies can often find excellent opportunities to address market segments in which their capabilities provide competitive advantages. We have already noted Nucor's outstanding record in steel. James River Corp. found excellent growth opportunities in the paper industry. Fifteen years after its founding, its sales exceed $2 billion, and it earned a superior return on equity. Crown Cork & Seal Co. compiled an outstanding record of growth by concentrating on conventional tin cans and bottle tops while larger can makers were investing in other areas. Between 1968 and 1978, Crown's earnings per share increased by 312 percent, while American Can's grew by 42 percent, Continental's by 17 percent and National Can's by 25 percent.

Of course, investing in entirely new fields can be rewarding too. But in considering such investments, a company has less reliable information than when evaluating activities in which it has already demonstrated it can earn an attractive return. This inherent risk must be taken into account when considering investment in industry in which a company has little experience.

## RETURNING CASH TO INVESTORS

The principal alternative to reinvesting funds generated by operations is to return cash to investors. Money is put into a company because investors expect that eventually more cash will flow back to them than they invested. Hopefully, every firm eventually reaches a point where it can reward its shareowners. Management must determine the timing, amount, and form of such payments.

Senior executives have usually had little to do with dividend decisions as they were progressing through the ranks. Their experience provides little help on dividend policy. So they look to the company's past practices, to what other companies do, or to conventional wisdom. As in other aspects of management, these sources of guidance frequently lead to errors.

Taking a broad view of the issue and applying common sense reveals the basic considerations to take into account. When a company has attractive opportunities to invest all of its available funds in projects that project attractive returns, it should reinvest its cash. Funds it cannot reasonably expect to invest at a superior rate of return it should return to the shareholders who have a wide range of investment opportunities open to them.

Unfortunately, managers frequently fail to see when to return cash to the owners. Most companies pay less than half of their cash flow as dividends, regardless of the return they could achieve by reinvesting the funds. Many companies with excellent investment opportunities pay cash dividends to shareholders at the same time they are raising capital from outside the company at considerable cost. Others continue to plow the bulk of their cash flow back into operations that offer little prospect of attractive returns.

Humana Inc., a leading hospital management firm, has continued to develop excellent investment opprtunities. Over a five-year period, it grew at an annual rate of about 25 percent. Earnings averaged over 25 percent on equity, suggesting that its investment opportunities were outstanding. It financed its growth by issuing over 11 million new shares and borrowing over $500 million. At the same time, it paid out over 25 percent of earnings as cash dividends to shareholders! It could have reinvested all of its earnings advantageously, spent less of raising outside funds, suffered less dilution of stockholders' equity, and permitted shareholders to avoid paying ordinary income tax on well over $150 million of cash dividends.

U.S. Steel exemplifies the company that continues blindly to invest in unattractive operations. For 20 years, that corporation demonstrated that it was unable to earn a satisfactory return on what it was doing. Nevertheless, it followed a policy of pouring more and more money down the same rat holes. During the 70s, it reinvested approximately three quarters of its cash flow in its existing businesses. Its capital spending was approaching $1 billion annually! The shareholders (and the economy) would have been far better off if the company had returned that cash to the owners to invest in more promising ventures.

Why do corporations adopt cash dividend policies that are not in the stockholders' best interest? Any of a wide variety of factors can lead management to make poor decisions about dividends.

Dividend policy is influenced more by custom and conventional wisdom than by an analysis of shareholder interests. A study I conducted several years ago showed that most companies listed by Value Line paid between 10 percent and 40 percent of earnings in cash dividends. Many of the others were in industry groups such as utilities where higher payout ratios were customary. Management and directors are reluctant to deviate from accepted practices. And often their investment bankers recommend conformity with custom.

Companies often try to enhance their stock price through dividend policy. To give stockbrokers a better story to tell prospective customers, many firms try to build a history of steadily increasing dividends over a period of years. Financial advisors frequently recommend such a policy as a way of making shares more attractive.

It is doubtful whether such a practice actually leads to higher stock prices. Convincing evidence is lacking. For a company with attractive growth opportunities, financial performance can be enhanced by reinvesting the cash rather than paying it out as dividends. Higher dividends either sacrifice opportunity or occasion extra financing expense. Earnings would thus be higher if the company paid no dividends. The theory that the investing public will pay more for shares of the company if it follows a dividend policy leading to inferior earnings growth is questionable at best.

The personal interests of the CEO can affect dividend policy. Corporate growth brings prestige and financial rewards to top management. High cash dividends limit the financial capabilities of a company to expand. Executives would usually prefer investing most of the company's available cash in attempts to grow rather than paying the money out to shareholders. On the other side, CEOs of smaller companies with excellent growth prospects sometimes institute cash dividends feeling that such action gives them more status in the business community. Moreover, some CEOs with substantial equity in their companies raise the dividend rate in order to increase their own current income.

Stockholders often press management for dividends even when they clearly would be better off without them. Through inheritance or misguided purchases, some investors who need current income acquire shares in companies that have never paid cash dividends and whose policy is correctly to reinvest all of their cash flow. Even at annual meetings of high-growth companies earning an excellent return on capital, one hears shareholders pressing for a higher cash dividend. (Such companies could mitigate this problem by briefly stating its dividend policy in each annual report.)

When a company's cash flow exceeds its investment opportunities, management faces the question of how best to return cash to shareholders. In the United States, a corporation can pay cash dividends or buy in its own shares. Most other developed countries have legal impediments to a company reacquiring its own stock.

Buying in shares is often more advantageous to stockholders than paying cash dividends. The owner can choose whether to sell and thus to create a taxable event. Depending on what he paid for the stock, he may not incur any income taxes at all if he elects to sell. If he does incur a tax, it will probably be at the more favorable capital gains rate. He may elect to hold the stock, the value of which should be enhanced by the retirement of other shares. Some investment analysts look favorably on any company with a program to buy in its own shares. Whether a stock repurchase plan is actually more advantageous than cash dividends depends partly on the price of the shares and on the impact of the plan on corporate control. It certainly merits consideration as an alternative to cash dividends.

Blindly conforming to convention or following the advice of outsiders with respect to returning cash to investors can be a disservice to shareholders. As in other management functions, vision is needed to determine the best policies. And as elsewhere, looking carefully at the impact of alternative courses of action can help develop that vision.

We saw in the last two chapters how computer modeling can contribute to sound financial planning. DSS can help determine optimum dividend policy as well as how best to allocate capital among operations. Regular use of this technique can help even executives with no financial training to gain insight into the effect of different types of financial policies.

Financial policy should be an integral part of a company's game plan. Executives who approach the subject in that spirit can often find ways to improve corporate results measurably, and to reduce basic risk as well.

# PART 3

# VARIATIONS ON THE THEME

# 11

# Small Companies

## OPPORTUNITIES AND PROBLEMS

People often think of corporate size as analogous to that of an athlete: the small competitor has the odds against him. In professional basketball or football, there are few ordinary-sized players, and those few have had to be unusually skillful and quick to make the grade. Similarly, people often assume that small companies can survive only by being quicker and more flexible than their giant competitors. Small businessmen who lack confidence in their agility quake when faced with competing with corporate behemoths. They expect to be trampled to death in short order.

This kind of analogy is unfortunate. Business is not an athletic contest. There is more than one game in town. In some activities, such as mass producing automobiles, enormous resources are necessary to succeed. In others, such as washing cars, smaller firms can do very well. When I was a manager at GE, I was impressed with how assiduously the company avoided direct competition with small business. The executives were terrified at the very thought of competing with "alley shops."

In athletics many relatively small individuals excel. They play badminton, perform gymnastics, run the marathon, ride race horses. In these sports, the larger competitor is at a disadvantage. In business too there are many areas in which smaller firms have an edge. Big companies are not well suited to running machine shops, dry cleaning establishments, custom plastics fabricators, or acting as manufacturers' representatives. The trick is to find the right businesses in which to compete.

When they acquire other companies, large corporations often overlook the fact that in some businesses, size can be a handicap. They buy successful small companies only to see them go sour after the acquisition. Frequently, they have no alternative but to divest the operation at a loss later on. Sometimes, the original owner repurchases his operation at a fraction of what he sold it for and returns it to its former prosperity.

The stereotype of the successful small company has it competing in narrow, highly specialized businesses. True, many small firms succeed in just such areas. But the opportunity for small companies is much broader and includes manufacturing standard products at low cost as well. Nucor's steel joists and bars are low-cost, commodity- type products. The large industrial supply manufacturer described in Chapter 6 was losing market share to smaller competitors in the most standardized, lowest-priced segment of its business, not in specials.

What small companies can do in commodities is illustrated by Unifi, a producer of texturized polyester yarn. Founded in 1971, Unifi went up against the likes of Monsanto, Celanese, Hoechst, Phillips, and Rohm and Haas. These giants were more integrated and had far greater resources. But by keeping its operations simple and focused, Unifi was able to minimize administrative costs. Recognizing the critical importance of having the most efficient manufacturing equipment, Unifi repeatedly replaced older equipment with the newest machines. Larger competitors opted to make do with the old. Within a dozen years of its founding, Unifi was the largest, most successful producer in its field. By contrast, Celanese, despite its size, was unable to compete and quit the business.

Stryker Corporation is closer to the usual stereotype of the small company competing successfully with corporate giants. It is less than 3 percent of the size of competitors such as 3M, Pfizer, and Bristol-Meyers in the $2 billion orthopedics industry. Like Unifi, it has built the capability to do a superior job for its customers. It focuses on this single industry. It avoids both the risks of pioneering and the price competition characteristics of me-too products. Its talent is finding ways to improve and refine innovations made by others. By concentrating on what it does best, it earns a return on equity of well over 20 percent.

It often makes sense for small businesses to target market segments that are too small for large corporations to address economically. For example, Ralph Smykal, a home builder in Chicago, created a development catering to owners of private planes. The lots are clustered around a private airstrip owned by an association of residents. There is room enough for each owner to have his own hanger. We have seen other, more prosaic examples of smaller firms, such as Citytrust Bancorp, that have successfully positioned themselves in niches too small to be attractive to larger competitors.

There is no shortage of opportunities for small companies. As the examples just cited illustrate, there are many situations in which they can outperform larger competitors in producing standard products as well as in highly specialized market niches. What is essential is that they define their businesses clearly so as to have a reasonable basis for expecting to excel.

In addition to being more effective than larger companies in many established industries, smaller firms are better able to innovate than large corporations. Study after study has shown that R&D efforts in smaller companies result in far more innovation per dollar spent than such programs in larger organizations. Most revolutionary new products such as instant cameras, dry copiers, and personal computers have been pioneered by corporate midgets.

Successful innovation by small companies is not dependent on coming up with a blockbuster invention. A company can simply identify a promising new direction and systematically head toward it. For example, in the late 50s when the oil industry experienced tough times, conventional drilling became too competitive to be very profitable. Seeking to avoid the vicious competition there, drillers flocked to the emerging offshore market, which quickly became crowded too. One small company, Parker Drilling, saw a future in deep-well drilling and set about building competence in that area. By 1981, its special capabilities brought it over $500 million in sales.

In formulating strategy, executives of smaller firms face a different set of challenges from their counterparts in giant corporations. In some ways their task is easier, in others more difficult.

The CEO of a small company is closer to the real world of operations than the head of a larger concern. He is in daily contact with customers and suppliers as well as with his own operating people. He can see why orders are won or lost. He can observe what his firm can do better than others and what it does less well. He is better positioned than the head of a large corporation to see his company's basic economic functions and how well it is performing them.

This intimate familiarity with what is going on enables the heads of many small businesses to position themselves advantageously without formal strategic planning. The task of integrating various functional perspectives can be done much more efficiently when one person is in touch with all aspects of the business. He does not have to arrange for communications between various organizational units or try to interpret opinions and data originating elsewhere.

Being actively involved in day-to-day activities is also a potential disadvantage. The incessant demands for attention to a myriad of operating details can swamp a person. A small company CEO must concern himself with customers, supplier relations, personnel, taxes, government regulations, and the whole gamut of operating problems.

A privately owned firm does not have to worry about how its stock price will respond to the quarterly earnings report. But in place of that problem are concerns about cash flow. If like most, a small company is undercapitalized or growing or both, maintaining enough working capital to support needed inventories and receivables and still pay suppliers soon enough to keep their support is a constant challenge. Management must keep a sharp eye on the financial condition of large customers; a delay in collection can precipitate a crises.

These constant operating and financial pressures make it difficult for an executive in a small business to avoid a serious case of management myopia. He often finds himself on the competitive treadmill, running frantically just to stay even. Sometimes his view of the world becomes warped, and he begins thinking of himself as alone amid unreasonable and uncooperative employees, customers, suppliers, and bankers. His game plan is no more than to keep struggling and hoping for better times.

Small firms have a more pressing need than larger ones for strategic planning. They need a strategy to avoid head-to-head competition with companies of similar size and to avoid straying into fields for which larger corporations are better suited. They need to be more sensitive to possible adverse future developments because they have fewer weapons with which to combat them. They have a greater need for planning because their financial resources are more limited. But they have little or no staff to focus on that type of work.

The fundamentals of strategic planning are the same for any firm. But the management of a smaller company must clearly recognize the special problems related to its size when it addresses the practical problems of dealing with the company's future.

## STRATEGY FORMULATION IN A SMALL FIRM

The key to successful strategy formulation for any company is to understand what strategy is all about. Senior management must recognize the central importance of defining its business so as to enable the firm to equip itself better than others to serve its markets. In a small firm with fewer resources, management simply uses different methods to get the job done.

Executives in many small firms are skeptical about the practical value of carefully defining their businesses. Conceptual activities seem too theoretical to have a tangible positive effect on operations. Yet a clear strategy has a pervasive influence on decisions at every level. It can contribute at least as much to a small enterprise as to a large one.

Formulating strategy requires information about markets, competitors, the business environment, and the company's own capabilities. In a larger company, elaborate programs are needed to collect, organize, and analyze such data. In a small firm, the situation is less complex. Top management is, or at least should be, closer to the market and in a position to see the opportunities and risks the company faces. It simply needs the ability to stand back and see its situation objectively, to identify the areas in which the company can expect to build competitive advantage. It has the facts. It needs to put them into perspective.

For example, a little company called Sharper Image has built a remarkable record of growth and profitability in the mail-order catalog business. Its success stems directly from the founder's definition of his business. He has described his target market in detail: an affluent man in his mid-30s with a fondness for gadgets, exercise, and a bit of ostentation. When one of his buyers proposes broadening an offering, the CEO says, "We're not in the business of offering choices. We're in the business of selecting for people." This clear vision of his economic role resulted in sales skyrocketing from 0 to $85 million in five years with an average sale triple that of most other catalog merchandisers.

The same approaches a larger company might use to develop vision are available to a smaller one. It can estimate the return on capital it is already earning in its various market segments. The CEO can get experience in looking objectively at corporate situations by serving on other boards. As he sees opportunities available to other firms, he becomes more aware of those available to his own. There are opportunities in all parts of our dynamic economy. The challenge is to see them.

One of the last places one would look for opportunity in today's world of solid-state electronics is in old-fashioned electron tubes. Richardson Electronics, Ltd., not only did very well as a distributor of electron tubes but in 1981 began manufacturing them. As large corporations such as Westinghouse and RCA got out of the business, Richardson got in. For most of what it makes, it is the sole source. While many entrants in glamorous parts of the electronics industry such as personal computers, disk drives, and floppy disks were losing money and going bankrupt, Richardson was averaging over 28 percent on equity. It tripled sales in a five-year period.

Germanium Power Devices followed a similar course successfully. Early in the history of solid-state electronics, some thought germanium would be a major raw material. Ultimately, silicon won out and germanium was relegated to a few, narrow applications. As larger companies that had invested in the field abandoned it, Germanium Power Devices bought the operations at low prices. The result was a very successful business.

In a smaller company, it is often the CEO who identifies and defines attractive opportunities, evaluates them, and establishes a plan to go after them. But a task force approach can be as useful there as in a larger corporation and for the same reasons. The special insights and knowledge of a functional vice president can be extremely valuable in formulating strategy. Moreover, involving a group in the strategy formulation process can build support for whatever decisions are made and broadens the vision of the participants.

When a CEO makes it clear that he welcomes this kind of activity, it is likely to occur even without designating an official task force. An informal approach sometimes results in activity more directly responsive to the needs of the situation than a more rigid, structured system.

The flexibility of the smaller company can facilitate experimentation as an approach to strategy formulation. If a company conceives of a new type of eatery such as a Howard Johnson's or a McDonald's, it can try out the idea on a small scale, modify it, and keep changing things until it has the right formula. Then it replicates the successful model and becomes a big company. Once a corporation is large, it is likely to acquire a more rigid organization and way of thinking, which makes experimentation with important new ideas more difficult.

Character is probably more important in the management of a small business than in a large one. When a small company such as Parker Drilling defines a business such as deep drilling, it must establish a plan to move in that direction. It must begin building the special capabilities needed for success in that field. For a small company with limited resources, maintaining continuity in such an effort, especially when things are not going well, is very difficult. It requires a CEO with vision who is committed to the strategy to see it through to a successful conclusion. He must enlist the active support of his associates by helping them see the opportunity and how to exploit it. And he must give it the priority it needs when money and manpower are in short supply if the program is not to founder.

## LONG–RANGE PLANNING

A *Business Week* article (January 9, 1984) on Pfizer Inc., included a photograph of the chairman with a stack of plan books from 23 of his divisions. The pile towered about four feet above the table on which it rested. And that wasn't the whole story. The article stated that over 30 of these books were created each year during Pfizer's six-week strategic planning exercise.

While this enormous stack of paper may serve a useful purpose for a $3.5 billion Pfizer, it clearly is not the way for a small company to go. Yet as we saw in the medical instrument company described on page 131 in Chapter 10, small companies must plan, too. Otherwise, they court disaster.

Whenever there is a question about a major decision, and this includes fixing the annual budget, the management of even a small company should consider its implications under various assumptions. As we have seen, a personal computer, even one costing $2,000 including software, can facilitate this activity. But even without data processing equipment, one can explore the possible long-term implications of proposed moves.

For example, a growing company may be pondering a $1 million expansion to its plant. It needs to determine where it can get not only the $1 million for fixed assets but also the working capital needed to support the additional volume. It needs to examine the cost of alternative sources of capital and the impact on the firm's financial flexibility for some time in the future. It needs to consider the implications of a cost overrun, a delay in completing the project, or failure to be able to sell the output. It must look at the possible effects of a future recession or of price erosion. It needs to consider the possibility that other, more attractive opportunities may come into view and to determine the effect of this expansion on the company's ability to exploit them. It needs to project long-term organizational requirements with and without the new facilities. For years, well-managed small companies have been doing these things without a computer. But a computer can help.

The CEO is responsible for considering various possible scenarios. He may assign the job of developing specific projections to a planning department, if he has one, or to his financial staff. In the case of very small companies, he may have to do the work himself. In even the smallest company, he must envision the entire range of reasonably possible scenarios and evaluate their implications.

In tiny companies, chief executives continue to scan the horizon for opportunity and danger informally and alone. As their companies grow, they begin to enlist the participation of others in the process. Eventually, the increasing complexity of both situations and organizations make it desirable to commit the plans to writing.

Long-range plans relate to three management activities. One is the annual budget. A second is specific major projects. The third is building general strategic capabilities. Written plans, especially in a smaller company, should be directed to these practical purposes. They should identify and briefly describe alternative scenarios. They should highlight key issues. Ultimately, they should provide insights into such questions as:

- If we plan to support Development X at a certain level and the economy goes sour, what is the likely result? How much worse off will we be than if we had planned a lower level of spending?
- If we reduce spending, what are the implications with respect to our short-and long-term competitive position?
- What are the risks and benefits of various levels of staffing under alternative sets of assumptions?
- Under what sets of circumstances will we lack the facilities, people, or money needed to take advantage of attractive opportunities that may be available to us? Or even to survive?

A small company cannot afford to generate elaborate planning documents as Pfizer does. Neither can it afford to plunge ahead without looking at the implications of what it is doing. A systematic attempt to see the broad outlines of future possibility can be crucial to a company's progress even if the alternatives are described only briefly or not at all in writing.

## FINANCIAL PLANNING

Much of the quantitative side of financial planning is taken care of in the modeling done in an effective long-range planning exercise. In it, management deals with how much money it will need under various assumptions, where it may be obtained, and at what cost.

As a company grows and changes and as new methods and equipment become available, it is appropriate to change financial procedures and organizations. Financial experience and knowledge can be crucial to determining when and how to develop the finance and control capabilities of an enterprise. If these are not available within the management of a small company, it can draw on the knowledge and judgment of its directors, bankers, accountants, or consultants.

Management should also consider qualitative aspects of financial planning. Relationships and reputation in the financial community affect the availability of funds to a corporation. Smaller firms especially need to develop the confidence of commercial bankers and perhaps investment bankers as well. To build credibility, they should avoid extravagant forecasts that may not materialize. By being frank and open with their bankers, they can build trust. The support of financial institutions can be a key factor in a company's ability to seize an opportunity or to weather an economic storm.

Developing a creative and flexible approach to financing can expand possibilities open to a small company. For example, Ferrofluidics, Inc. was able to pursue a potentially lucrative technical development through the use of an R&D partnership. Later, as the project scaled up, it was able to arrange a second-round financing through an imaginative scheme that permitted guaranteeing that investors would get 100 percent of their money back regardless of the success of the project.

As closely held companies get older, ownership often becomes dispersed among second-and third-generation family members. The financial objectives of various shareholders are often incompatible. Disagreements about financial policies are common. Some need current income and demand higher dividends. Others, especially those involved in management, want to reinvest available cash to build the company. Frequently, when ownership is divided among several family groups, none has control. Family relationships often make it more difficult to resolve such problems in a businesslike manner. Without leadership, the firm drifts aimlessly until it founders or is sold.

Principals of family companies can avoid such debacles through planning. By foreseeing likely effects of deaths and inheritance, company leadership can provide for orderly succession of ownership and management to the benefit of all concerned. Some family companies have found it very useful to have a lawyer, banker, or other person the owners all trust serve as a director to help guide the company and to avoid squabbles.

## PITFALLS

### Inadequate Capital

The most common cause of failure among small firms is inadequate capital. Inexperienced entrepreneurs underestimate the time and money required to get their businesses off the ground. They misjudge how long it will take to win customers. They do not foresee how much working capital will be required.

Financial crises are not limited to new companies. We have seen how an overly aggressive expansion program destroyed a promising medical equipment enterprise. Others have gone down the drain because of recessions, high interest rates, foreign competition, competitive developments, or adverse changes in the industry.

Sound financial planning can often avert such problems. Projecting financial needs is straightforward. But for one with little experience in the area, it is easy to misjudge or overlook important requirements for funds or to fail to take into account the kinds of developments that can spell trouble. Directors, accounting firms, banks, or consultants can help with foreseeing cash needs and determining how best to provide for them. With their assistance and a commitment to look at the full range of reasonably possible scenarios, a small company can usually avoid a financial crisis.

### The Competitive Treadmill

An entrepreneur often starts a new company in the industry in which he has been employed. He may have some approach to doing the job better than his former employers. Or he may simply set up to do the same thing in the same way, knowing some customers he can expect to capture.

A small firm's competitive edge may soon disappear. The new enterprise is beset with a myriad of start-up problems, while established firms move to diplicate or surpass its innovation. The young company may lack the money or the development expertise to come up with an encore to it first offering. Soon it finds itself in the same boat with a lot of other struggling firms, without a basic economic reason for existence. It is on a competitive treadmill it may find impossible to escape.

Avoiding this condition requires a commitment not just to being in business but to finding a unique economic role in which to make a special contribution. Management needs the vision to see the futility of doing what others can do just as well. It needs to recognize the difference between a better idea for a new product and the capability to create better products on a continuing basis. With only the former, it may be more profitable to license or sell the idea to a company that has the ability to exploit and build on it successfully.

## Growth

We have alluded several times to the firm that attempted to expand beyond what its financial resources could support. Money is not the only requirement for growth. Companies need technology, distribution, raw materials availability, manufacturing expertise, market information, and many other capabilities. Most of all, they need management.

As a company grows, its managerial needs change. It goes through a number of stages. At first, companies have only one manager, the chief executive. He directs the actions of all of the employees. At some point, he is no longer able to handle every problem himself and hires a professional staff: heads of manufacturing, marketing, financial control, and perhaps engineering and personnel. A growing company eventually outgrows such a simple functional organization and may divide operations under division general managers.

At each transition from one phase to another, there is serious danger that the company will outgrow the competence of the CEO. With each step, managerial needs change. Individuals who have succeeded as entrepreneurs or as heads of small operations often become set in their ways. They have learned so well what contributed to their early success that they are unable to throw off old habits and to adopt new methods and attitudes better suited to a more complex situation.

When small companies think about expansion, they should carefully consider their management resources. As it is difficult to be objective about oneself, the CEO would do well to consult experienced outsiders who are acquainted with his managerial skills. Unfortunately, executives with the wisdom to seek advice are the ones who need it least.

Growth entails other risks. In many ways, small companies are attractive places to work. Each individual has a sense of personal worth that is largely absent in larger corporations. There is less bureaucratic restraint. As a company grows, it often looses good people who dislike the increasing formalism of a larger organization.

Growth can turn the heads of management. Successful growth companies, and some which are not so successful as well, build fancy offices and acquire limousines and corporate jets. Some investment analysts see such signs as reason to recommend sale of shares. By contrast, one of the smallest, barest offices I have ever visited was that of Robert Noyce, Chairman of Intel, during the period of its spectacular growth. Analysts sensitive to the dangers of profligate spending should have done very well with that stock.

### Diversification

The difficulty of earning money is often less apparent outside one's own industry. Distant fields appear greener. Especially when they are on a competitive treadmill, companies may seek to improve their situation by diversifying. They attribute their poor results to conditions in their industry rather than to their own failure to develop a distinctive competence to serve any part of the market better than their competitors. They see other companies diversifying apparently successfully. So they try it themselves.

The lure of diversification is particularly hard to resist for a small firm with unique new technology. It may have potentially attractive opportunities in many different markets, far more than it can possibly exploit. Unless it is selective and concentrates on a few areas in which it can build a defensible leadership position, it may end up with nothing but memories of what might have been.

The danger of diversification for high-technology companies is discussed in Chapter 14. Special management problems facing any diversified firm are reviewed in Chapter 13.

At this point, suffice it to say that diversification is particularly dangerous for a small firm. It makes a company more difficult to manage. By adding complexity, it leads to higher overhead. It has led to the downfall of many a fine little business.

# 12

# Mature Industries

Most companies find themselves in mature industries. The overall economy is expanding at only 3–4 percent annually, despite the spectacular growth in areas such as electronics, robotics, and biotechnology. Clearly, most industries are expanding slowly or not at all.

The rate of change of a mature industry is typically slow. Its characteristics and trends are well established and well recognized. Innovation is limited primarily to exploiting new technologies thrust upon it from outside or to changes in marketing and distribution. Companies in mature industries focus on refining well-established processes in a continual struggle to make small gains in efficiency. After decades during which employees have moved from one competitor to another, there are few secrets. Each firm operates much as the others, plodding away on its treadmill.

Executives in such firms typically look to the conventional wisdom for a way out. They strive to gain the largest share of the market, sometimes triggering a price war. Not more than one achieves market dominance. Even then, it may show only mediocre results like those of U.S. Steel, Goodyear Tire, Alcoa, or Georgia Pacific. Such companies integrate vertically. They diversify. They emulate other companies. But results continue to flag. Ultimately, many become part of a sordid dramas such as Carborundum/Kennecott/Sohio/BP or Bendix/Martin Marietta/Allied.

It does not have to be that way. Companies in mature industries do not have to accept the role of being clones of the industry leader nor to accept poor results. Many firms in mature industries are top performers. They have developed unique arrays of capabilities that provide them with competitive advantages in their particular market segments. They are important contributors to our country's economic health.

Securing significant competitive advantages in a mature industry is not easy. But in a business arena that does not change rapidly, a favorable position, once achieved, can often be maintained for a long time. Companies such as Procter & Gamble, General Cinema, Clorox, Dow Jones, Fort Howard Paper, Nalco Chemical, Dennison Manufacturing, Delux Check Printers, Maytag, Illinois Tool Works, R. R. Donnelley, Meredith, and many others just keep churning out attractive earnings year after year, decade after decade. They do much better than most companies in more dynamic environments that are vulnerable to abrupt changes in the market or in technology.

Generating attractive results in a highly competitive, mature industry requires vision and character. It requires seeing and facing up to the harsh economic realities of the situation. It requires a sound game plan. More than elsewhere, it requires:

1. Identifying and building the capabilities that can contribute most to improving efficiency and effectiveness rather than to growth.
2. Finding innovative ways to define market segments in which to facilitate building competitive advantage.

Mature industries often afford excellent opportunities for creativity. However, rather than new products and new applications, the most important innovations in mature industries are likely to be aimed at efficiency, productivity, and quality. Many American "smokestack industries" are suffering because they continued to use old methods while the Japanese introduced new, more efficient methods of production and quality assurance.

## MANAGERIAL FOCUS

In a mature industry, it is especially important that executives recognize that their primary responsibility is to get the most out of the resources at their disposal. The temptation to diversify can be hard to resist. An obsession with growth can be fatal.

The idea that profit opportunities in older industries are scarce is a myth. An analysis of the most recent Fortune 500 companies when this was written showed that the six industries providing the highest return on equity were:

1. Tobacco.
2. Publishing and printing.
3. Pharmaceuticals.
4. Soaps and cosmetics.
5. Food.
6. Beverages.

Office equipment, including computers, was in the lower half of the industries listed.

Kellogg Company, for example, demonstrates what can be achieved in a stable business environment. Its leading products have been around for over a quarter of a century. The rate of growth of cereal consumption has been low and declining—demographics are against it. Yet Kellogg continues to earn an outstanding return on capital—higher even than IBM. For the 10 years 1974–84, Kellogg's earnings growth rate and total return to investors was about the same as IBM's. At the time of this writing, Kellogg's price-earnings ratio was better than IBM's. And Kellogg's performance has been far better than its competitors in the food industry who pursued growth through diversification. Kellogg focused on the ready-to-eat cereal business and has built superior capabilities to serve that market.

Another company that has done well in the food industry is Campbell's Soup. The CEO has a fetish for keeping management in close touch with the market place. He insists that his executives do their own grocery shopping and does so himself. He has even held a board meeting in the back room of a supermarket and then arranged for the directors to roam the store and to talk with customers about Campbell products. Based on unusual sensitivity to the buying preferences of an ever-changing market, Campbell's Soup has been able to come up with a raft of new products catering to specialized market niches. It offers ethnic and other specialized foods for regional markets. Its Vlasic Foods subsidiary has even geared the flavoring of its pickles to the different tastes of customers in the various regions of the United States. Campbell's Soup's return on equity is consistently high despite having relatively low debt.

An obsession with growth in mature industries is especially dangerous. Finding expansion opportunities in the field they know best is difficult. So executives feel *compelled* to enter businesses for which they are not properly equipped.

That attitude was reflected in an article on Mattel in *Business Week* (May 9, 1983). "Mattel Inc. is stuck between a rock and a hard place," it began. "Children's infatuation with electronics is *forcing* the kingpin toy maker to diversify away from what it knows best—making conventional toys, including the hugely successful Barbie doll line—into the less familiar and faster-paced business of consumer electronics."

One can picture the thoughts of Mattel executives when they decided to go into electronic games. "It's the wave of the future." "If we don't go electronic, our competitors will leave us in the dust." "It's the only way we can grow." "Without electronics, we'll die on the vine." So they created Intellivision and plunged into the melee.

As the article in *Business Week* pointed out, this was a different kind of business. In consumer electronics, product cycles are short. Product development in the new business was different. Intellivision bombed and had to be abandoned. In just one year, Mattel's net worth plummeted from $275 million to *minus* $136 million. The company was nearly destroyed.

Ironically, Mattel's mature lines saved it. They continued to do well. Based on their performance, the company was able to raise additional capital and to restructure its balance sheet. But the cost to the original shareholders, whose stake in Mattel was badly diluted, was enormous.

In hindsight, it is quite clear that Mattel was not forced to go electronic. It would have done much better if it had stayed out of electronic games altogether. The only thing that made it go into electronics was the ubiquitous obsession with growth. Blinded by the temptation to expand into an exciting new field, management could not see the hazards there. It found excitement, all right, but not the kind it sought.

The kind of corporate culture and management style appropriate to a company in a mature industry is sharply different from what is needed in a more dynamic environment. In a high-technology company, what is critically important is to move rapidly and in the right direction. Achieving a technical lead over the competitors is more important than trimming manufacturing costs. It makes sense to spend heavily on technical talent and on creating an environment in which they can be effective. But in a mature industry where change takes place more slowly, operating efficiency and expense control are often crucial.

Efficiency calls for specialization. We saw in Chapter 1 how Chase Brass became the top performer in the brass mill industry by severely curtailing its product line and gearing its plant to manufacture standard items at minimum cost. AFG Industries has done the same thing in the flat glass industry When AFG chose that strategy, it dropped its two largest customers because they involved too many special orders. When others crowded into metallic-coated glass, a high-margin specialty item, AFG got out. It went after window glass, a commodity item costing a tenth as much. Management understands it is in a highly competitive, mature industry in which the decisive factor is manufacturing cost. By focusing on the key issues, efficiency and productivity, and trimming out all of the unnecessary fat, AFG has done much better than many of its larger competitors.

Older companies often find this hard to do. Over the years, expenses for management and indirect labor tend to grow. From time to time, companies have gone after new product opportunities until their lines become too broad for optimum efficiency. Owners and directors have tolerated mediocre results and worse. Many of America's smokestack industry companies have become vulnerable to more efficient competitors. They have been sitting ducks for the Japanese.

In the machine tool industry, for example, the Japanese focused their efforts on the smaller, more standardized products typically used in job shops. Aided by government guidance and research support, they developed highly efficient production of technically advanced machines. Their invasion of the American market was like the German conquest of France in 1939. Against weak resistance, they quickly gained a major share of the segment of the market they attacked.

In recent years, many large companies have sold poorly performing divisions in mature industries to the unit managers through leveraged buy-outs. In the typical scenario, the new owners drastically cut the size of the management staff and other overhead expenses immediately. Spurred by the need to meet heavy interest payments and relieved of the need to go through various exercises required by the staff of the former parent, executives take aggressive actions as owner-managers that they did not do as employee-managers. Their change of status has imparted to them a clearer vision of how the business should be run.

**BUSINESS DEFINITION**

In a mature industry, where there is little or no growth and where competitors are probing every corner of the market for opportunity, a carefully formulated strategy is essential to success. Clear product differentiation, as between Apple and IBM personal computers, for example, is rare. To define a unique role as a basis for building competitive advantage, management must be more closely tuned to small differences in customer needs and buying habits. Retailing and distribution provide a wealth of examples of successes and failures based largely on the finesse with which managements segmented their markets.

In the early days of discounting, K mart, then S. S. Kresge, was only one of many to enter the field. The concept was efficiency in mass marketing, cutting out all of the frills in order to deliver merchandise to the consumer at the lowest possible price. Many of the entrants achieved initial success based on that definition of their business. But as the industry grew, they lost sight of their basic economic role. They saw customers who wanted a broader line from which to select, fancier fixtures, more and better sales clerks, and charge accounts. So they tried to broaden their appeal by becoming more like a conventional department store with its higher cost structure. They gradually dissipated their competitive advantage. But K mart remained true to the discounting concept. It kept efficiency and cost reduction as its first priority. By developing a superior capability in this vital area, it compiled one of the most remarkable records of any enterprise ever. Others such as Woolco, Korvettes, Two Guys, and Mammoth Mart dropped by the wayside.

More recently, K mart has begun losing its focus too. Management has felt the usual compulsion to keep growing. Because expansion opportunities in the business as originally defined seemed limited, it decided to broaden its line. It has added higher markup, impulse items to take advantage of the traffic through its stores. Initially, the new strategy seemed to pay off. But customers are learning that no longer can they be confident that they will return from shopping at K mart with the best buys around. It will be interesting to see whether the new game plan works in the long term or whether it is a merely short-sighted liquidation of K mart's reputation for value.

Another successful discounter is Caldor. Its business definition is more subtle. Its target is the price-conscious, middle-class department store customer. Caldor's costs are lower than the traditional department store, but its ambiance and service are different from K mart, whose customers tend to be blue-collar workers. The difference is so significant that one analyst has said, "Caldor and K mart are not even in the same business."

Zayre Corp. has been successful in still another segment of the market. Many of its stores are in inner-city areas. It has catered to a low-income clientele and to minority groups. The chain made a "significant commitment to become very good at something that (other retailers) were running away from," according to its president. The inventories of its inner-city stores are tailored to the special needs and tastes of area residents. Zayre too has generated excellent returns.

Dollar General Stores targeted still another segment of the discount retailing market—small towns. It keeps expenses down by operating out of cheap storefronts and having few sales clerks. It specializes in production overruns and discontinued items. Although it sells primarily on price, its net margins are double those of K mart. Earnings per share have grown at about 20 percent per year. Dollar General isn't the only retailer to have aimed at small towns. Wal-Mart, Family Dollar, and Ames Department Stores have targeted similar markets and have all done extremely well. Wal-Mart compiled an incredible record of sales and earnings growing at over 35 percent per year for over 10 years—in retailing.

Opportunities abound at the other end of the price spectrum too. Nordstrom Inc., a West Coast chain of specialty stores, caters to a more affluent clientele. Its sales clerks, who earn up to $50,000 per year or more, lavish personal service on the customer. Its stores carry enormous inventories and can fit a person of almost any size or shape. Costs are high and so are prices. Between 1974 and 1983, Nordstrom's profit rose from $5.2 million to $40.2 million, an annual growth rate of 25 percent!

The same kind of opportunities are open in the distribution business. Newark Electronics, for example, targets small maintenance and repair accounts that its larger competitors regard as a nuisance. Their average order is only one fourth as large as those of a leading competitor. But Newark has tailored its operations to that market segment. Its salesmen even get referrals from other distributors who don't want to be bothered with small orders.

Newark has been the major contributor to the outstanding record of earnings growth of its parent company, Premier Industrial Corp.

Anixter Brothers, Inc. distributes wire and cable. It was founded on the concept of saving customers the time it would take them to locate special items they needed. It carries a very broad inventory and features immediate deliveries. Providing superior availability of wire and cable is a simple business definition, but the company is almost alone in its field. By selling convenience, it gets a good price for its products. The fact that it is a mature business hasn't kept it from growing rapidly—it soon will be a billion dollar corporation!

The list could go on and on. Earlier, we saw examples of successful companies in other mature industries including steel bars, brass extrusion, banking, industrial supplies, and business forms. What these companies have in common is a focus on a segment of the industry in which they have equipped themselves to excel. They have had managers who have had the vision to select a specific economic role to play and have built an outstanding ability to fill it.

Because such vision is unusual, companies with a sound strategy can grow even in mature industries. But that should not divert attention from the fact that industry overall is not growing rapidly. Our economy needs managers who can improve efficiency and productivity, even where sales volume is declining. As Peter Drucker wrote in *The Wall Street Journal* (December 30, 1983), "If it is no longer realistic to say: 'We plan to double size within 10 years,' then the goal has to be: 'We plan to double our productivity within 10 years'—of capital, of key physical resources, and of people at work. Improving productivity is always a realistic goal and can always be done."

In the same article he pointed out that "Opportunities will knock on the doors of even a stagnating industry," and "Managing the no-growth company requires asking all the time: 'What are our strengths? And where are there new opportunities to apply them productively, whether because of changes in population and demographics, or in markets and distribution, or in technology?' "

The kind of thinking Drucker recommends was exhibited by Action Industries, Inc. In 1981, it was a chain of 32 stores selling hardware and housewares. It had never been very profitable. However, the company had been consistently successful with its "Dollar Day" promotions. The Chairman decided that Action was better at promoting sales than at retail operations and liquidated the stores.

Three years later, the company had sold its retail outlets and was solely in promotion and wholesale. It designed ads and provided merchandise for retailers including giants such as K mart and Sears. Earnings in fiscal 1983 were already more than twice what they made in their peak year as a retailer.

Furniture is one of the oldest industries in America. Yet one furniture manufacturer, Herman Miller, Inc., was able to convert itself into an emerging growth company. It has stayed in its traditional field, office furniture, and retains the same family management and corporate culture it has had for generations. But it spotted the trend toward open-plan offices early and led the move in that direction. Over the decade 1975–85, the company's earnings grew at almost 25 percent per year and were expected to exceed 20 percent on equity in 1985.

The pitfalls faced by executives of companies in mature industries are the same as those faced by their colleagues elsewhere. But they are harder to avoid and can be more serious. It is more common for firms in stagnant industries to get locked onto a competitive treadmill and have their visions clouded by management myopia. If they feel compelled to grow, to diversify, to take a fling at an emerging industry, the risk of disaster is much higher. Attuned to the needs of a stable environment, they are not equipped to deal with a rapidly changing business.

The procedures for strategy formulation, long-range planning, and financial planning in other types of businesses are also applicable to companies in mature industries. But especially high priority should be put on methods for developing vision, countering management myopia, and avoiding an obsession with growth. When management can see its business in broad economic terms, define an area in which it can excel, and focus on doing that job well, it can achieve success in terms of creating value for all concerned. And, as we have seen, one of the incidental results may well turn out to be healthy growth.

# 13

# Diversified Corporations

Despite the dismal record of diversification as a business strategy, the conglomerate is a potentially sound corporate form. The record of Textron under Royal Little, of Teledyne under Henry Singleton, and of General Electric under a long series of CEOs demonstrate that highly diversified companies *can* succeed. It has been the failure of management to define the economic role of the corporation when it diversified that has led so many to grief.

The objectives that prompt many companies to diversify are unsound. When the reasons for it are wrong, a diversification program is unlikely to produce favorable results.

## RATIONALIZING DIVERSIFICATION

Perhaps the most common motivation for diversifying is the obsession with growth. Commenting on CBS overpaying for a group of magazine properties, *Forbes* magazine (December 31, 1984) said, "Why is CBS taking a chance? Call it desperation, almost. Growth is slowing or stopping in its major businesses." The article went on to review CBS's past record of "spending on anything offering a hope of growth: an expensive cable-TV culture channel, a videodisc plant, an in-house film company, a paperback book publisher, stereo stores on the West Coast. So far these are all losers." This same feeling of being forced to diversify almost destroyed Mattel, as we saw in Chapter 12.

It's the old story of using inability to do well in the field a company knows best as a rationale for trying new areas. A management committed to growth above all else tries to rationalize

175

such moves. But when one looks objectively at such a course of action, he quickly sees that it is unsound.

A second major driving force behind the compulsion to diversify is concern about the vulnerability of a single-industry company. Never mind the superior record of focused companies. Never mind the risks inherent in entering unfamiliar businesses. Managers can see more clearly the risks closer to home, *especially if they lack confidence in their ability to cope with the risks in their own industries.* Managers are attracted by the apparent security of diversification. If one business goes sour, others (hopefully) will do well enough to assure the continuing profitability of the firm.

From a broad economic point of view, it is difficult to conclude that conglomeration results in an overall reduction of risk. Investors can obtain the benefits of diversification more effectively and at less cost by purchasing securities of a variety of firms themselves. Workers in shrinking industries are vulnerable to layoffs, whether employed by a unit of a conglomerate or by an independent company. Moreover, as we have seen, diversification itself is fraught with danger.

Nevertheless, this notion of safety in diversification pervades the business community. So much so that financial institutions have even been able to sell what *Forbes* magazine called "The dumbest idea in years"—mutual funds that invest only in other mutual funds. Piling management fees on top of management fees, they trade on the notion that since diversification is good, double diversification must be better.

In recent years, the benefits of "portfolio management" have been cited to justify collecting dissimilar operations in a single corporate entity. The claim is that this arrangement facilitates the transfer of investment from one unit to another, a so-called "redeployment of assets." But our economic system has proven quite able to redeploy assets without relying on conglomerates to do the job. It is not at all apparent from the record that having diversified corporations shift investment from one industry to another is either more efficient or more effective than the other mechanisms. Companies in shrinking industries can pay large dividends, buy in their stock, sell assets, or go through partial or total liquidation. Deserving enterprises in expanding fields have little trouble finding interested investors.

Others claim that aggregating a number of operations in a single corporation enables it to raise capital at less cost than they could do as independent entities. In some cases, this is true. However, the most common reason for needing additional outside capital is rapid expansion. When one sees the price-earnings ratios commanded by many small growth companies, it is hard to believe that being part of a larger corporation would provide access to equity on better terms.

## COSTS OF CONGLOMERATION

Whatever advantages, real or imaginary, are claimed for diversification, they must be weighed against the disadvantages. We have already cited many examples demonstrating the risks inherent in diversification. We have also cited the work done by Boston Consulting Group demonstrating that increased size and complexity leads to *increased overheads per unit*. One aspect of this effect can be illustrated in a simplified chart representing a conglomerate organization:

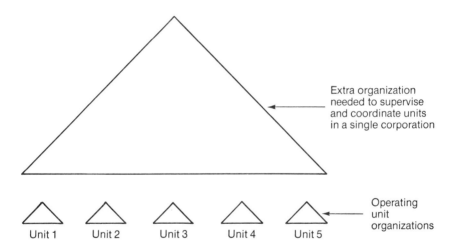

The highest paid, and often least productive, members of the corporate organization are found in the triangle at the top. When the units are independent enterprises, that heavy overhead burden is avoided. Not only is the extra superstructure expensive, but it generates additional work in the operating units and reduces their ability to respond quickly to changing conditions.

Another cost to the investor is the low value the market assigns to the shares of many diversified companies. Their prices would often be even lower if investors did not recognize the possibility that there companies may be a takeover targets. Astute corporate raiders often see an opportunity to profit by dismembering a company to realize the intrinsic value of the individual units. For example, in 1981, Marvin Davis and Marc Rich paid $722 million for Twentieth Century-Fox. Immediately, they broke the company into marketable pieces including a Coke bottling franchise, real estate, movie theater chains, resorts, and land development operations. By selling these assets, they were able to drain about $1 billion out of the company over the next three years while still retaining the film studio. After taking over 100 percent ownership, Davis was able to sell half of the remaining entity for another $250 million.

Because the stock of diversified firms so often sells at less than the value of their component units, managements feel compelled to assign high priority to preparing defenses against takeovers. They might better be more receptive to the underlying message the market is sending them: Their game plans are fundamentally unsound. They are in more businesses than they can manage effectively. Their shareholders, the individual operating units, and the economy as a whole might be better off if the corporation were broken into more sensible pieces. But, of course, this would threaten the status and compensation of corporate top management, so it is rarely done.

Years ago, as a stockholder, I wrote to the CEO of General Electric Company suggesting that he split up the company. He graciously sent a long, detailed response. He wrote that the separate pieces could be more valuable than the whole only if the GE corporate office were not cost-effective. This possibility he quickly dismissed as unthinkable. Management myopia?

## A RATIONALE FOR CONGLOMERATION

How do all of these negatives square with the first sentence of this chapter that says that the conglomerate is a potentially sound business form? The answer lies in the definition of the role of the corporate office of a diversified company. It can be worth more than its cost if it can provide for better management of its operating units than they would likely achieve as independent enterprises.

Management quality varies widely from one company to another. As we have seen, management myopia is widespread. In addition, senior executives in many firms lack the skills, talent, or character needed to be fully effective. As a result, the potential of many corporations goes unfullfilled.

Our economic system relies on boards of directors to govern corporations. Their role is not to manage operations but to provide for effective management of the enterprise. But directors are notorious for their failure to meet that responsibility. They are reluctant to replace management except in a crisis situation. The norm is to tolerate mediocre performance indefinitely. And in closely held companies, there seldom is a board worthy of the name. When management has control, it is in effect accountable to no one.

The result is that many independent companies are managed poorly. Under these circumstances, a corporation such as ITT under Harold Geneen can buy almost any kind of company, install tight controls, discontinue losing operations, sell surplus assets, and show excellent results. The economic function of the acquirer is to do what directors should have been doing already: to provide for good management. Improving operations pays excellent dividends. But if a corporation buys too many companies or if it acquires operations that are too dissimilar, it will eventually have trouble providing for good management of operations on a continuing basis.

This is what happened at ITT. Mr. Geneen has candidly stated, "People always ask me how we selected the things we acquired, and I can tell you exactly: What was available." He had the ability to increase the profits of his acquisitions after he made them. But ultimately, ITT became an awkward hodgepodge with no clear business definition. Performance deteriorated until it became obvious that the separate parts had greater value than the company as a whole. A new management began to sell off pieces in an effort to trim the corporation down to a more manageable size. It was identified as an attractive takeover target for someone who might dismember it more rapidly.

But given the shortage of good managers and the usual ineffectiveness of boards of directors, there is a place in the economy for a conglomerate. In effect, its corporate office can substitute for boards in the various divisions. It selects and supervises unit chief executives. It oversees and may participate in strategy formulation and long-range planning. It sets financial policy and raises capital. It provides and helps develop broad vision for the operations. It controls the allocation of capital between the operations.

Well-managed conglomerates govern their divisions better than most boards. They do not tolerate mediocre general managers. If the head of a division does not produce, and does not respond to efforts by the corporate office to help him do better, he is replaced. Many diversified corporations require their units to maintain tight financial control, to have strategies and plans, and to build resources for the future. Boards of directors of independent companies are seldom thorough in requiring sound management practices.

If there is a sound rationale for conglomerates, why aren't more of them successful? Very few have done well over a long term. I felt challenged to name even three successful examples to use in the first paragraph of this chapter. Not one of the 62 "excellent" American companies identified by Peters and Waterman in *In Search of Excellence* is classified as a conglomerate. Looking at the record of companies listed in the "Multiform Industry" section of Value Line is hardly encouraging.

There are many reasons for the generally poor performance of conglomerates. One is the difficulty of providing for effective management of operating units. Selecting and supervising general managers and helping them to correct weak areas in their operations is a challenging task requiring unusual talent. Business schools do not teach that skill. Successful unit general managers fail at top management as often as successful salesmen fail at sales management. Senior executives often yield to the temptation to try to manage the operating units, rather than providing for good management. The corporate office often becomes so involved in the business of acquiring new units and selling ones that have gotten out of control that they lose sight of their primary responsibility of taking care of what they already have.

The risks inherent in acquiring and the costs inherent in complexity apply to even the best-managed conglomerate. Those that attain a measure of success rarely know when to stop. The corporate Peter Principle usually prevails. Successful acquirers just keep on buying until they have more than they can manage. Even new managements, which see the problems resulting from the excessive diversification of their predecessors, are soon back on the acquisition trail after they have sold a few losers. The cash realized from the divestitures seems to burn holes in their pockets. Ultimately, they suffer from the higher overheads and rigidity of any large, complex organization.

This tendency of other conglomerates to go too far and to create an unmanageable hodgepodge of operations is what makes the Bairnco approach (see p. 41, Chapter 4) so interesting. A small, talented group of senior executives should be able to acquire and add substantial value to a series of companies by doing a superior job of governance. The key is to spin the units off as independent companies once competent management is in place. A company committed to such a course would have an enormous advantage in recruiting general managers: They could look forward to being CEOs of independent companies. For the reasons mentioned above, the corporation should arrange for strong boards of directors of the spin-offs to maintain effective governance after the units become independent. This is especially important if instead of distributing shares to the corporation's stockholders, it sells them to the public to obtain funds for further acquisitions. The record of these divestitures as independent companies will affect the value of future spin-offs.

In the face of increasingly effective international competition, it is important for American industry to improve the quality of its management. Some diversified companies have demonstrated the ability to improve the managements of what they acquire—for a time. Eventually, even the best of conglomerates, like Textron, become too diversified and complex to perform well. Thus the Bairnco concept of *processing companies*, improving them and spinning them off, is one which merits further exploration.

## MORE MODERATE DIVERSIFICATION

Moderate diversification is far more common than conglomeration. In some ways, the management problem is even more difficult.

In a single-industry company, top management makes the key operating decisions. Its knowledge of the industry and judgment about what to do are the best in the company.

When a company diversifies through acquisition, the best knowledge and judgment about the new field are usually in the management of the acquired unit. Even when a new business is developed internally, it often takes years for top management to learn the business.

In a newly deversified company, top management is accustomed to making the key operating decisions. It still thinks of itself as the proper group to run the operations. It finds itself in a position like being a little bit pregnant. It is not yet ready to make the transition from actively managing operations to providing for effective operating management. It is not qualified to manage its newly acquired businesses. Having had no experience doing it, it is not equipped to exercise hands-off supervision of general managers either. It is betwixt and between, neither fish nor fowl. And usually it does not even recognize the problem.

What is the proper role of the corporate office of Exxon when it diversifies into electronics? Or of Schlumberger when it buys Fairchild Camera, a semiconductor manufacturer? Or of Texas Instruments when it tries to get into consumer products? When the typical company diversifies, management fails to see the need for a fundamental change in the definition of the business and, with it, of the role of the corporate office. So top management continues to make the key decisions. And unless the top executives are unusually astute, they make serious mistakes.

Ultimately, top management may learn to understand the new buisness and what kind of general manager it needs. The time required depends on the executives involved and the degree of diversification. Also, after a period of time, management may learn how and when to delegate more of the decision-making responsibility to operating executives. At Ventron, originally a materials company, it took me perhaps five years and a succession of general managers before a reasonably successful relationship with our new activities in instruments was achieved. As a director of Tech/Ops, I have had the opportunity to watch the CEO, after years of problems with diversification, become skillful in managing such dissimilar activities as personnel monitoring services, radio broadcasting, and industrial equipment manufacturing. It is significant that in both cases, the chief executives, faced with the serious problems of managing diversification, decided to cut back the scope of their companies' operations to make them more manageable.

## MANAGING THE DIVERSIFIED CORPORATION

The first requirement for managing a diversified corporation is to recognize the special needs of that type of enterprise and to define the role of the corporate office appropriately. The greater the diversification, the more top management must play a role like a good board and provide for effective operating management, rather than engaging in it.

Corporate offices of successful diversified firms are usually small. Larger staffs are more likely to be drawn into operating decisions, justifying their existence by telling unit managers what to do. Unless top executives have special expertise in the specific business, and often even then, making operating decisions at the corporate level is likely to be a mistake.

Top management of a diversified corporation must select and supervise general managers. This is no small undertaking. The CEO

---

### PRECEPTS FOR DIVERSIFIED CORPORATIONS

1. Recognize the special needs of managing diversity.
2. Focus on bringing superior general management to operating units.
3. Keep the corporate office small.
4. Develop the ability to supervise general managers.
5. Develop outstanding competence in finance and in financial control.
6. Build a capability of identifying and evaluating acquisition prospects in light of the company's ability to enhance the value what it buys.
7. Develop an ability to structure deals that appeal to the needs of the particular sellers while remaining attractive to the buyer.
8. Learn when and how to sell operations that do not fit.
9. Require each operating unit to have a well-defined strategy, sound plans, and effective financial controls.
10. Determine actual and potential return on capital in each segment of the corporation and allocate resources accordingly.
11. Limit efforts to develop synergistic advantages to one or two key areas such as technology or marketing, and even then, only when the potential advantages are compelling.
12. Be sensitive to the different effects of corporate culture and management style in different businesses. Avoid policies, procedures, and directives that may make it more difficult for each unit to be responsive to the unique needs of its particular market.
13. Limit the scope of diversification to businesses top management can learn to understand before accepting serious risks.

---

must recognize that the company's progress will depend on his building that capability in the corporate office. He must work continually to that end, improving his own skills and those of any subordinate group executives. Directors can sometimes provide assistance, provided the CEO is not above soliciting help from his board. But this is a field of managerial activity about which there is little organized knowledge.

The corporate office must see that the business of each operating unit is defined and that each division formulates appropriate strategies and long-range plans. Ideally, corporate management will help unit managers develop the ability to do those tasks effectively themselves. But where capable operating executives have limited vision, corporate executives may have to continue indefinitely to provide guidance in the direction they should pursue. Objectivity and experience may enable top management to help set strategy. But it must stay out of day-to-day operating decisions.

Finance is a key function of the central office of a diversified corporation. Financial planning, raising and allocating capital, and financial control are critically important. Corporate accounting should arrange for developing information on the return on capital in every part of the business. It should provide data to help the CEO evaluate the performance of each activity and decide what to build and what to shrink. The CFO should prepare financial plans covering the whole range of potential developments to help the CEO decide how to structure the balance sheet, what risks he can afford to take, and how much financial flexibility he must maintain. The CFO needs to find the most advantageous ways to provide for the availability of additional funds and to raise capital when it is needed.

Another critical skill in running a diversified company is deal making. Management must be able to identify and evaluate acquisition prospects. The key issue is the ability of the buyer to add value. It is nearly always a seller's market: Prices paid for companies are typically far higher than the value placed on them by the stock market. Unless the buyer can increase the earnings of what it buys or the acquired operation can somehow increase the earnings of the acquiring company, the investment is unlikely to produce an adequate return—unless the buyer can sell pieces of the acquisition for more than it paid for the whole.

Successful acquirers must be able to find ways to structure deals so as to satisfy the needs of both buyer and seller. Unusually creative financial executives and/or investment bankers are critical resources for the diversifying corporation. Finally, the ability to be persuasive—to find the seller's "hot button" and convince him that the offering is the most attractive he can expect to get—is essential. For a conglomerate, building superior deal-making skills can provide a critical competitive edge.

Unfortunately, many diversifying companies have focused far more attention on deal making than on developing the special skills needed to manage a multiindustry company. Buying companies is much more glamorous than running them.

Managing an acquisition program requires seeing the overall situation as well as the individual deals. At Ventron, uncertain whether our narrow technological base would provide opportunities to employ our management or our financial resources fully, we decided to diversify. We bought 10 companies. In each case, we did a reasonably good job of evaluating opportunities and risks. But we completely misjudged the difficulty of managing all those units together. Fortunately, we woke up in time, sold some units, and consolidated what remained into a simpler organization. As we narrowed our focus, I could feel the company becoming more manageable and more profitable, month by month. After the fact, I realized that what we had undertaken had had the potential to destroy the enterprise.

No matter how astute the management, it may acquire operations it cannot run well. Management must be able to recognize and to admit that it has erred and to divest such businesses promptly. It is helpful to have, or to have an investment banker who has, the skills to divest advantageously. Seeing the need to dispose of an operation and having the discipline to do it promptly is much more important than getting top dollar for it. Putting money and effort into trying to build value in a loser is almost always a mistake.

As it gathers experience in acquiring and in trying to enhance what it has bought, a management with vision will refine the definition of its business. It will learn the characteristics of activities it can run well and of those it cannot.

In defining the business of the corporation, the CEO will be tempted to reach too far to exploit potential synergistic interactions between operating units. In companies that focus on a single market or single technology, such opportunities may be worth pursuing and may even be the central unifying concept of the enterprise. But in a highly diversified corporation, efforts to force collaboration between units often fail.

As a salesman for GE, I frequently found myself in a customer's lobby with one or more other GE representatives whom I didn't know and had nothing to do with. I have frequently heard such circumstances described as crazy, a profligate duplication of effort. But when a company burdens salesmen with too broad a line or hires additional people "to coordinate" the efforts of the various representatives, cost-effectiveness usually suffers. The GE system of decentralization in which operations operate quite independently has worked well.

Diversified corporations frequently spend large sums to establish a corporate identification as a synergistic advantage. They hire a consultant to design a distinctive logo, prepare a graphics manual, and require all operating units to conform to it. Typically, ads will carry the signature of both an operating unit and the corporate parent, confusing the audience and dampening the impact of the message. Corporations spend huge sums on institutional advertising in an effort to make the public aware that a leading brand of luggage is made by the same entity as a well-known line of lamps, for example. They hope such programs will add to the value of their shares and, incidentally, perhaps help move some merchandise. What actually results is more like the director in the blue serge suit who wet his pants in a board meeting. He got a nice warm feeling, but no one else noticed.

Companies frequently run into problems when they diversify, even within a single industry, in order to pursue apparent opportunities for synergism. When the notion of one-stop shopping for financial services swept the industry, there was a rush to combine insurance, banking, stock brokerage, real estate, and other activities within a single corporation. Some of the unhappy results are described in Chapter 15. For years, freight handlers have conceived of synergistic advantages of combining road, rail, water, and air transport into a single system, but companies that have moved in that direction have realized little benefit from it. Long ago, many of the container companies diversified to be able to offer cans, bottles, boxes, and plastic containers. Results were poor, and most of them have spun off major parts of what was once their grand strategy. As we saw earlier, the one company that stuck to its knitting, Crown Cork & Seal, performed far better than its competitors that diversified. But as recently as 1983, National Can bought several glass bottle plants, still looking for the elusive synergism among different types of containers.

Executives should realize that many synergistic opportunities do not require common ownership of the participating operations. The value of a technical development is sometimes greater when exploited by a well-qualified outside firm than when handled by one of the company's own divisions. Stores often find it more profitable to have certain departments run by concessionaires rather than using its own employees and capital. Any business function including research, development, manufacturing, or sales can sometimes be best handled by outside companies.

When companies diversify they must be sensitive to differences in corporate culture and to the need for different management styles in different industries. In a highly diversified corporation, central management must be unusually flexible in permitting each unit to use the type of management that best fits the needs of its industry. Even in a conglomerate, however, top management will inevitably impose certain values and behavioral norms on operating units. Corporate management must be perceptive enough to recognize what these are and to limit its operations to industries in which its basic approach will enhance rather than retard the effectiveness of the units.

Shortly before this was written, General Motors acquired Electronic Data Systems. The cultures of the two organizations contrasted sharply. EDS had a more aggressive and innovative management style. The compensation practices of the two firms were quite different. EDS rewarded excellent job performance with large bonuses and merit raises; GM salary increases were automatic. EDS had a strict dress code prohibiting beards among other things.

GM transferred some 10,000 of its white-collar workers to EDS. The culture shock caused serious problems. Some GM employees quit. Others sued. Still others talked about organizing a union.

GM management seemed to be committed to trying to blend these two disparate cultures into a unified corporation. Whether this would be possible and, if so, whether a common culture would be effective in the two dissimilar industries, seemed questionable. Whether the merger would bring the desired results clearly depended importantly on how management defined its business and the role of the corporate office. A central issue was whether the new GM was to be a diversified corporation with different units having different styles or a single unified company with a single culture. It appeared that if management persisted in the latter approach, trouble lay ahead.

## DIVERSIFICATION AND VISION

To managers without vision, diversification is a way to grow when the company's existing business is stagnant. It is a way to reduce risk by spreading it over several businesses. To many such executives, it has proven to be a short cut to trouble.

Diversification is a risky business. It creates a company that is harder and more expensive to run than a more focused firm. Yet some unusually talented managements have demonstrated that diversified corporations can be successful.

Royal Little, who pioneered the concept of the conglomerate with Textron, saw clearly that his new creation was a unique corporate form. He defined the role of the corporate office and developed the capabilities needed to acquire advantageously and to improve the management of the operations he purchased. Seeing the need for a coherence of approach and skills even in a conglomerate, he limited Textron's scope to manufacturing concerns. He consistently produced a return of over 20 percent on equity.

Succeeding managers at Textron lacked Mr. Little's vision. They went into other types of operations including financial services. They failed to do as good a job at providing for excellent management of operations. Textron's performance and stock valuation declined. Finally, faced by the threat of being taken over, the company merged with Avco, another conglomerate.

For an executive with vision, diversification is an alternative meriting consideration. But he must realize that it inevitably involves serious risks and added management costs. He must realize that managing diversified operations is fundamentally different from running a company serving a single market segment. He must see the need to develop and recruit superior line managers and to delegate day-to-day decision-making to them. He must understand the unique role and needed capabilities of a corporate office of a diversified company and work continually to develop excellence in the key areas.

For a talented executive with the vision to see clearly what is involved in managing diversified operations, that route can be rewarding. But managers who diversify simply because they are not satisfied with the results they can achieve in their own industries are on thin ice. Usually, they simply add to the long list of disappointments resulting from failure to see what diversification really means.

# 14

# High-Technology Businesses

High technology is the darling of the business world. Otherwise astute businessmen eagerly throw millions at emerging industries. Big companies like Exxon, GM, and GE pour billions into electronics and robotics. Venture capital itself has become a multibillion dollar industry. Successful high-technology entrepreneurs such as David Packard, William Hewlett, Edwin Land, and Steven Jobs dot the list of America's richest people and most famous industrialists.

The passion for high technology, like malaria, is a recurring phenomenon. In the late 60s, it was rampant. In 1968, for example, Ventron Corporation floated a stock offering at $68.50 per share when it was earning only about $1. Other high-technology companies, many of which had never made a profit, were selling at multiples of sales volume. By the early 70s, the mania had subsided. Many deserving firms could not find public financing at any price. A new wave of enthusiasm crested in the early 80s and then ebbed again.

Large companies, eyeing the phenomenal success of companies such as Intel, Apple Computer, and Lotus Development seek to participate in such opportunities. They invest heavily in research, buy small, high-tech firms, or set up captive venture capital operations.

As we have already indicated, when promising technologies are identified, they attract so much capital that the average return is poor. For every Apple, there are scores of lemons. Even experienced, successful venture capital firms expect many of their investments to go sour. Each new industry is characterized by hopeful entries swarming in followed by a shake-out period that decimates the ranks of fledgling ventures. For example, in the mid-80s, most manufacturers of personal computers, disk drives, floppy disks, and software were in difficulty and not expected to survive. Most of the genetic engineering firms too were suffering losses.

While high-technology industries sometimes provide opportunities for spectacular success, they are inherently risky. The technologies and the market are in continual flux. Forecasting demand is almost impossible. Powerful, new competitors suddenly appear on the scene. Just as quickly, companies disappear. When a major customer or supplier fails, it can be catastrophic to a start-up venture. In high-technology industries, inability to define a sound economic role results not just in confinement to a competitive treadmill but more often in outright failure.

## CHARACTERISTICS OF HIGH-TECHNOLOGY BUSINESS

Much of industry, including old-line businesses such as transportation, mining, and even agriculture, employ sophisticated, new technology. What is different about high-technology business is the emergence of new *markets* in which technical sophistication is a primary determinant of success. It is the growth of markets driven by technological change that is the unique mark of a high-technology industry.

A number of other characteristics derive from the basic nature of this type of business. High-technology companies employ a lot of engineers and scientists. Facilities, organization, and corporate culture reflect the number and importance of technically trained personnel. Production costs are relatively unimportant. (Yield, however, is sometimes critical. In making certain integrated circuits, chemicals, and pharmaceuticals, only a small percentage of the output meets specifications. Yield improvements can dramatically reduce costs and can determine whether an operation is economically viable.)

Because high-technology products usually have high unit value, shipping costs are relatively unimportant. At the same time, most high-technology companies need ready access to specialized suppliers and services and to particular skills that may only be available in certain regions. Companies of this type tend to congregate in areas where engineers and scientists like to live and where an appropriate infrastructure, including a leading university, is available. Silicon Valley in California and Boston's Route 128 are obvious examples.

Financial services are an important part of the necessary infrastructure. A study contrasting the development of high-technology companies in eastern Massachusetts with the lack of the same in Philadelphia attributed much of the difference to the greater support of the financial community in Boston.

High-technology companies are usually founded by engineers or scientists. Many fail to appreciate the importance of marketing, finance, or general management. As a result, many new high-technology firms are one-sided and flounder when they fail to maintain decisive technological leadership. Even technical prowess, unless it is overwhelming, may not be enough. Soon after IBM introduced its PC, others introduced computers that were technically more advanced. Despite their attractive product features, they were unable to compete successfully. Other factors were more important.

High-technology business is pervaded by change. Technology keeps changing and with it, markets. The business environment keeps changing. For example, the outstanding success of the IBM PC soon make it difficult to sell a personal computer based on any other operating system or diskette size, regardless of technical merit. Increasing public sensitivity to safety hazards changed the rules of the game for many industries from atomic power to waste disposal.

Not only external changes but internal ones as well can be critical. Changing technologies and markets require changes in priorities and activities. These factors, together with rapid growth, necessitate wrenching organizational realignments. High-technology companies are often crippled by a lack of management talent capable of coping with such a dynamic situation.

Market development is a critical factor in a high-technology business. Initially, potential customers are unaware of the new products. After they learn about what is available, they may still be ignorant about how to use the new items. Frequently, they need to change their way of operation in order to take full advantage of the new technology. People are reluctant to abandon procedures that have served them well in the past. The success of a high-tech enterprise frequently depends on the skill with which it teaches customers how to use its products.

Exploiting new technology to create new products for new markets is risky. Especially when success in each of several areas such

# PITFALLS IN EMERGING HIGH-TECHNOLOGY COMPANIES

*Ownership and Control*

1. Partners and/or investors with ill-defined or incompatible objectives.
2. Failure to define and agree on a viable business role for the venture.
3. Failure to recognize the need for competent general management and integration of all functions.
4. Unrealistic expectations of immediate success.

*Financial Management*

1. Undercapitalization
   A. Underestimating the time required to generate positive cash flow.
   B. Failure to recognize all of the capital and expense factors involved.
   C. Failure to recognize working capital requirements of rapid expansion.
2. Sources of Financing
   A. Use of inexperienced investors.
   B. Use of inappropriate forms (e.g., short-term borrowing to finance long-term projects).
   C. Failure to build constructive relationships with sources of money.
3. Control
   A. No budget.
   B. Inadequate expense control.
   C. Little or not knowledge of costs.
   D. Poor credit management.
   E. Lack of inventory control.

*Marketing Management*

1. Assumption that product will sell itself.
2. Ignorance of the size and nature of the markets and competition.
3. Assumption that customers will readily alter established practices to use the product.
4. Underestimating established competitors.
5. Pricing too low to support needed marketing, technical service, and new product development activities.

6. Pursuing too many different markets.
7. Failure to provide for adequate sales support, such as sales literature, technical service, and field maintenance.
8. Use of improper or conflicting channels of distribution.
9. Overoptimistic forecasts (followed by unpleasant surprises).
10. Failure to provide adequate after-sales service.

*Product Development*

1. Bringing product to market before development is complete.
2. Product proliferation.
3. Inadequate product definition; continuing alterations.
4. Inadequate specifications; poor basis for quality control.
5. Poor productivity.
6. Hard for customer to use the product successfully.
7. Keeping developments in the lab too long, striving for perfection.
8. Failure to provide for continuing innovation.
9. Excessively ambitious technical goals.

*Summary*

1. Assumption that technology alone will carry the day.
2. Failure of investors and managers to agree on objectives and business definitions.
3. Failure to provide adequate business management of all functions.
4. Failure to plan.

as technical development, manufacturing, and marketing are all necessary for success, the chances of failure are great. If the probability of success of each of three essenuial elements is 60 percent, the chances of overall success is less than one in four (.6 × .6 × .6). Actually, there are a great many pitfalls into which a new high-tech venture may fall. Some of these are listed in the box on pages 192–193. We shall examine only a few of them in the balance of this chapter.

## RELATING TECHNOLOGY TO CUSTOMER NEEDS

The heart of high-technology enterprise is envisioning how new technology enables one to meet customer needs more effectively than was previously possible. Seeing such opportunities leads to the creation of whole new industries such as dry copiers, instant photography, solid state electronics, computers, and satellite communications.

Few people understand both technology and market needs well enough to be able to innovate successfully. Individuals such as Thomas Edison, who had the insight to see a broad range of possibilities, such as incandescent lamps, the phonograph, and movies, are rare indeed. Most successful high-technology companies, even giants such as Xerox, Polaroid, Intel, Wang Laboratories, and Digital Equipment, have achieved success primarily in a single field.

Pioneering enterprises are often founded by engineers with the insight to see a new market opportunity based on new technology. Whether they succeed depends not only on the quality of the basic idea but upon their ability to muster the total resources needed for an effective enterprise: leadership, money, marketing skills, and operating effectiveness. Other high-tech firms are spin-offs, formed by engineers from companies already in the field. They build on breakthroughs pioneered by others. They may start with an idea for a product improvement or a plan to target a particular market niche. In any case, the ability of the firm to market the product, to finance operations, to continue to upgrade its offering, to improve its products, and to find better and better ways to serve the customers is critical to its success.

In some cases, a gifted individual, often a founder of the firm, has so firm a grasp of technology and markets that he can continue to identify opportunities for innovation. Polaroid's Edwin Land and Wang Laboratories' An Wang come to mind as such persons.

Eventually, though, the flow of commercially valuable new ideas from the founder dries up. Finding a similarly creative successor is almost unheard of. If the company is to continue to innovate, it must institutionalize the process of relating technical possibilities to market opportunities. That is a challenging task.

Some firms such as 3M, IBM, Intel and Hewlett-Packard seem to have succeeded in designing an organization that continues to innovate and to create new business opportunities. Others such as Digital Equipment and Polaroid, which pioneered in new fields, manage only to retain their leadership positions as their industries mature. Still others fall by the wayside.

Without the leadership of a creative genius, success in technical innovation requires productive collaboration between inventors and marketers. The process is made more difficult by the fact that in today's complex world, both product development and marketing require teams of talented individuals. These groups must learn to communicate effectively with each other. The engineers must see and explain what is technically feasible and at what cost. The marketers must understand and explain what customers will buy and at what price. Together, they must arrive at a single, integrated vision of the opportunities available to their company.

Managing the process is not easy. It requires creating an environment or culture in which creative engineers, talented marketers, and hardheaded accountants can work together with mutual respect and understanding. It means giving individuals and teams enough freedom to innovate without permitting them to squander enormous sums on ill-conceived projects. It is a continual balancing act between encouraging innovation and accepting errors on one side and exercising enough control to avoid disasters on the other.

Chief executives of successful high-technology companies agree that theirs are people businesses. Of course, perceptive managers in any field recognize that their effectiveness depends on the performance of their employees. But in a mature industry, success is often tied to the creation of a well-defined *system* that does not depend primarily on the availability of unusually talented individuals or on complex personal interrelationships. It is more difficult to systematize innovation.

The participants in a new product development program inevitably see things from their own point of view. Engineers are most concerned with the technical aspects. They often show little interest in such necessary details as how easy or difficult it may be to manufacture the product, find raw material suppliers, set up quality control standards, provide in-service maintenance, or explain to the customer how to use the product. In some cases they are so committed to technical excellence in the product that they insist on approaches that are too costly or risky or time-consuming. Some researchers continue to see opportunities to improve a new product and keep it far too long in the laboratory.

Marketing people, on the other hand, see the shortcomings of what they currently offer and are in a hurry to have something new.

Responding to their pressure for speed, companies frequently introduce new products before they are fully developed or before manufacturing procedures or quality control standards are fully worked out. The results can be disastrous.

Years ago, the Revere Camera Co. proudly showed the first home movie camera with electric eye exposure control at an international exhibition of photographic equipment. Recognizing the potential marketing impact of the new item, Bell & Howell quickly organized a crash program to develop its own electric eye camera. It turned out that Revere's product was not yet ready for mass production, and Bell & Howell actually beat them to the market with volume shipments by many months. As Bell & Howell had realized, the innovation was a blockbuster. During the period when Bell & Howell was shipping and Revere was not, Revere's market share plummeted. It never recovered. Ultimately, it sold out to 3M. As a factor in the home movie camera market, it had destroyed itself.

What management can do to help avoid such mistakes is to develop a common understanding as to what constitutes a successful development program. It must represent an attractive value to the customers. It must be completed within time and expense budgets appropriate to the market. A new product must be completely defined including what raw materials to use, how to make it, and how to control quality. Good cost estimates are essential. Provision must be made for instructing customers how to use it and for maintaining it in use. There must be a plan for marketing it. All these steps are normally necessary before going public with a new product.

Management needs to develop a group feeling of responsibility for getting the whole project completed. Some companies employ product managers to coordinate development activities to achieve an integration of engineering, manufacturing, marketing, and financial control. Others create ad hoc task forces to work together on new product projects. What is essential in institutionalizing the innovation process is to integrate knowledge of what is possible with what customers need and to build a coordinated development program. Without the leadership of a creative genius, achieving effective collaboration of various functions requires a great deal of management talent and effort in a high-technology enterprise.

## THE NEED FOR FOCUS

One of the characteristics of high-technology businesses is usually a surfeit of opportunity. Companies with a command of a new technology see innumerable potential applications for their knowledge. The problem is that they lack the resources to pursue them all successfully. If they are to succeed, they must decide to pursue only a few and to abandon most others.

Too often a high-technology company, dazzled with the possibilities before it, "jumps onto its horse and gallops off in all directions." Rather than choosing just one, it aims at a group of targets and fails to hit any.

Developing a new market for a product or a technology is no small task. The supplier needs both the ability to sell to the industry in question and an adequate command of the technology of the application of its product. This implies an understanding of both economic and technical aspects of the customer industry. Successful market development often requires extensive application laboratories in which the supplier can simulate the conditions found in the customer environments. Such facilities are required both to determine what is needed for the application and also to be able to instruct the customer how to use the new product.

To do what is necessary to develop a variety of applications is an imposing task, even for a large company. In the early days of the silicone industry, for example, silicone oils, resins, and elastomers showed promise for auto and furniture polish, dielectric fluids, release agents, electrical insulation, sealants, mechanical rubber parts, masonry water repellants, and a host of other uses. Even General Electric Co., one of two early entrants in this field, saw that it did not have the resources to pursue all of these possibilities effectively. It decided to focus on silicone rubber, built its primary market position there, and achieved excellent earnings as a result.

Early in the history of the commercial development of sodium borohydride, Ventron was the only domestic producer. At that time, that company had total revenues of less than $2 million. It was pursuing about two dozen different potential applications, from stimulating oil wells to fuel cells to making cellulose more resistant to heat and age. Recognizing the impossibility of developing so many markets, the company decided to focus on just three. In hindsight, management wondered if it had cut back far enough. Developing markets for dyeing textiles, bleaching woodpulp, and purifying chemicals was already an ambitious undertaking for such a small firm.

By focusing its efforts, a company can build its technical competence into a formidable competitive weapon. After several years of commercial development, the application technology Ventron had accumulated in the three markets it concentrated on would have been very expensive for anyone else to duplicate. After more than a quarter of a century of commercial sales with volume running well into the tens of millions, Ventron was still alone in the field.

Eastman Kodak's technical strength in color film was for decades a similar barrier to entry by others. On one occasion, Du Pont had developed a product superior to what Eastman was then selling. It teamed up with Bell & Howell, a leading marketer of photographic equipment, to challenge Eastman in its area of greatest strength. Because it had developed so much technical expertise in this field, Eastman was able to reach into its bag of tricks and to introduce a superior product, Kodachrome II, which Du Pont was unable to match. Rather than launch what would have been a hopeless effort, Du Pont and Bell & Howell abandoned the project.

Some companies that concentrate on a single technology or product line are not as focused as they believe. If they are selling into a variety of industries, they need to develop information, application technology, distribution channels, and marketing competence to serve each of these markets. They may have to maintain technical staffs and application laboratories for each market segment in order to serve it effectively. This diffusion of effort can be enormously expensive and still leave a company vulnerable to attack by a more focused competitor.

## THE NEED FOR STRATEGY

It is important for the management of any company to be able to envision and select an economic role in which it can expect to excel. It is important too for management to consider potential future developments and to be prepared even for the unexpected. In the fast-changing environment of high-technology industry, that is especially difficult to do.

Predicting how a new technology will develop is extremely difficult. Even Robert Noyce, a founder of Intel and a pioneer in the field, was for a time skeptical about the long-term potential of integrated circuits in the early days of the development. Without a clear picture of what lies ahead technically, it is impossible to be confident about how markets will develop. Who knows where genetic engineering or space technology will lead?

But it is still necessary to make choices about both which technologies and which markets to develop. A company that tries to keep all of its options open, to cover the whole range of technical and market possibilities, will dilute its efforts so badly as to fail to achieve a leadership position anywhere.

To make these critical choices, management needs to develop a strategy. With the help of the best advice available, it must try to see the various threads of future technological development. It must try to relate these to market needs to see where the most attractive commercial possibilities may lie. It must realistically appraise competitors' and its own capabilities to see where it can reasonably expect to develop a competitive edge.

At the same time, it must give weight to present opportunities. Gambling on being able to hit a moving target years in the future is a high-risk game. Even if one guesses correctly, he may lose his financial support before reaching profitability. The best route to long-term success usually lies in the direction of activities that can also be profitable in the short run. As it develops, manufactures, and sells these products, it builds the capabilities needed to succeed with more advanced items in the future. The trick is to select current commercial opportunities that truly lie on the road toward attractive long-term potentials rather than on dead-end streets.

Management must always keep its company's uniqueness in mind. It is no good to choose the "correct" direction toward the biggest long-term potential if a dozen other companies, including those with greater resources for leadership, are pursing the same target. Each company must identify the specific objectives for which its own particular capabilities are best suited.

A new technology may open the door to many business opportunities. There are many markets in which it may find application. There are many areas of specialization within the scope of the new technology. In seeking to define the proper economic role for its company, management must seek to identify the particular combination of specific areas of the technology and specific segments of the market in which it can develop superior competence.

This kind of approach has characterized Advanced Micro Devices, one of the most successful manufacturers of electronic chips. It focuses single-mindedly on profits. It concentrates on a few specific market segments. It views technology not as an end in itself but as a means to make marketable products. Its chips sell for four times the industry average. Its returns on equity, growth rate, and stock price have been unusually high even for this industry. It has effectively married a primary concern for filling specialized customer needs with the required technical competence to do it.

In the same broad area of technology, Analog Devices has developed its own leadership position. It specializes in equipment for converting analog to digital signals and vice versa. Without attempting to compete with mass producers of standard integrated circuits, it manufactures special ICs for its own needs. Its management has shown unusual vision not only in its selection of technical and market targets but in building the human resources needed to carve an important leadership position in a segment of a larger industry dominated by corporate giants.

How does management acquire that kind of vision? The same techniques that work elsewhere are useful in high-technology companies.

First, top management must recognize that technical leadership alone is not enough to build a successful enterprise. It must define its business partly in terms of markets and of people and organization. Its distinctive competence must include the ability to identify customer needs and to deliver suitable products in a timely, cost-effective manner. Only if the CEO sees his enterprise as a business in which all functions are important, is he likely to achieve managerial vision.

He can broaden his viewpoint in the usual ways: exposing himself to business education, listening to competent outside business advisors, building an effective board of directors, and serving as a director of other companies himself.

Smaller high-technology companies have one special and potentially valuable source of advice: venture capitalists. Often maligned, and sometimes called "vulture capitalists," these financiers of young firms have a business orientation that engineer-entrepreneurs often lack. The better venture capitalists represent a potential source of seasoned judgment that can be more valuable to a fledgling company than the money they invest. They have contributed to the success of many outstanding, high-technology companies from Digital Equipment to Apple Computer. Long after those companies became large and financially strong, they kept their venture capitalists on their boards in recognition of the value of their counsel.

One of the contributions venture capitalists make to many high-tech firms is to insist on a sound game plan. They have seen how many fledgling companies fall into the pitfalls awaiting companies that plunge ahead based on technical skills alone. Whether or not venture capitalists are involved, high-tech companies need a strategy, a business definition that defines a viable economic role for themselves. Otherwise, the odds of failure are overwhelming.

# 15

# Service Firms

Services are now the largest segment of our economy and continue to grow year after year. Some of these activities such as health care, education, transportation, communications, and financial services represent major industries in themselves. Others such as maintenance and repair of industrial equipment are sometimes organized as adjuncts of manufacturing businesses.

The concepts and procedures presented earlier in this book are applicable in service businesses as well as manufacturing. Some of the examples already used, such as Citytrust Bankcorp and Frontier Airlines, have been drawn from service industries. The preceding chapters apply as much to service companies as to others. A service firm has as much need to define its businesses, to select market segments in which it can reasonably expect to excel, and to build superior competence to serve the targeted areas as a manufacturer. Management myopia is just as dangerous there as elsewhere in business.

But there are differences too. Service firms for the most part rely more importantly on interaction between their employees and their customers. Exact duplication of what is offered to the buyer is more difficult; specific individuals and locations, for example, are more often key elements in buying decisions. It is harder for a customer to evaluate competitive services than to compare products offered by different manufacturers. Buyers can more easily obtain detailed specifications of automobiles, washing machines, or cameras than of financial or medical services. For the latter, they must rely largely on subjective impressions of others and on personal experience, often obtained at considerable discomfort.

Reputation and convenience often become the critical factors in the initial selection of a service firm.

Professional service firms such as doctors, lawyers, accountants, and consultants are a distinctive group of enterprises, different from other service businesses as well as from manufacturing, mining, farming, or fishing. To begin with, many members of this group deny that they are businesses at all and reject the idea that they should be managed like a business. Traditional taboos against certain sales promotion techniques tend to distort competitive methods and to make it harder for customers to select suppliers intelligently. The collegial relationship between members of a professional firm can make it difficult for its management to organize a coherent program to target specific market segments, to develop capabilities in defined areas, or, in fact, to set any strategy at all. Established practices and attitudes can interfere seriously with a firm's economic results and with its effectiveness in carrying out its professional functions.

In this chapter, we shall examine different kinds of service firms. We shall consider how the concepts discussed earlier in this book apply to each situation. By examining different kinds of service business, we hope to help the reader see how to apply these ideas to other businesses as well, either in the service sector or elsewhere.

## FINANCIAL SERVICES

Financial services has become thought of as an industry comprised of commercial and investment banks, savings institutions, insurance companies, stock brokerages, investment management firms, accounting firms, trust companies, venture capitalists, consumer finance companies, factors, financial planners and advisors, providers of credit cards, and firms offering a wide variety of other services primarily involving money. Traditionally, firms in these fields specialized in only a small part of the total range of financial services. To some extent, this reflected legal prohibitions and to some extent the preference of these firms for specialization. Even within a group such as insurance companies, individual firms tended to specialize in one area such as insuring life, property, or health. Many specialized even more narrowly such as offering life insurance for members of labor unions or government employees.

With the maturing of the American economy and the intensifying preoccupation with growth, many of these specialized firms began expanding outside of their traditional fields. Life insurance companies billed themselves as financial planners. Accounting firms established management consulting arms. Thrift institutions began offering checking accounts. Banks adopted the slogan "a full-service bank." The general notion of a one-stop financial service vendor entranced more and more executives in the industry.

Government moves toward deregulation encouraged that kind of thinking. Soon major insurance companies such as Prudential and Sears Roebuck (Allstate) were buying large stock brokerages such as Bache and Dean Witter. Sears also bought a major national real estate firm. American Express, the largest credit card company, acquired an insurance company (Fireman's Fund), a mutual fund (Investors Diversified Services), a stock brokerage (Shearson, Hammill), and then an investment banker (Lehman Brothers, Kuhn Loeb). Merrill Lynch, the largest stock brokerage firm, expanded its investment banking activities and plunged into real estate. When it created its Cash Management Account (CMA), which integrated checking, credit card, stock brokerage and lending services, it began competing directly with banks. The largest bank, Citibank, developed a competitive service. Many other banks, already offering lending, checking, and credit card services, began providing discount stock brokerage services in order to compete with other types of institutions.

Rather than pursuing distinctive differences, financial institutions seemed to be striving to be more like each other as a provider of a wide range of financial services. Rather than focusing on carefully selected market segments, they were seeking to sell any product they could offer to whoever would buy it. Rather than building competence in specific areas in which they could hope to excel, they rushed like Merrill Lynch's "thundering herd" toward the common goal of offering customers every financial service they might want. Enterprises such as smaller banks, which lacked the resources needed to compete seriously in this insane race, accepted the notion that they could not survive in a world of financial service giants. Many began preparing themselves for sale.

Executives of these firms would do well to study the histories of the cockroach and the dinosaur. As we have seen over and over, size is not necessarily the answer to economic effectiveness or corporate success. In other industries, smaller firms continue to prosper by filling specialized roles. Experience elsewhere suggests that this will occur in financial services too. What is less clear is that there will be a viable place for even a single giant one-stop emporium of financial services. The dinosaur has disappeared while the cockroach lives on.

Early leaders in the race to become the largest, most diversified financial services firm paid dearly for their initiative. Prudential bought Bache in 1981 for $385 million. By 1984 Bache was losing over $100 million per year. Dean Witter plunged into the red after Sears acquired it. According to *Business Week* (June 18, 1984), "in broadening its products and services, Merrill Lynch lost control of its costs." In the fourth quarter of 1983, it reported its first loss since it went public 13 years earlier.

Perhaps the staunchest adherent to the concept of a financial services supermarket, American Express encountered troubles too. The losses of its insurance subsidiary dragged the parent's earnings into the red in the fourth quarter of 1983. Shearson's earnings, too, were down sharply. Eight months after American Express bought a European bank for $520 million, its chief executive, widely believed to be the bank's most important strength, left. An article in *Fortune* magazine (June 1984) accused American Express of using accounting gimmicks to conceal some of its earnings problems. The irony of the situation is that its traditional businesses were booming. Without the excess baggage collected in its effort to be everything in financial services, American Express would have shown outstanding results even with straightforward accounting.

Meanwhile, the small fry that continued to do what they did well remained healthy. A 1982 study by the Federal Reserve Bank of Atlanta found that small banks across the country had continued to gain market share. A senior vice president of one of America's largest banks explained, "The small banks have outsmarted us by going after specific niche markets. We have tried to be all things to all people, and that's made us vulnerable to target marketing." (*INC.*, May 1984). Some, like Citytrust Bankcorp., focused on small accounts where large banks have trouble competing. Others have found success in upscale banking, providing customized services for affluent individuals. In the recession year of 1984 for brokerage business, A. G. Edwards of St. Louis was making good money, while the big Wall Street firms like Merrill Lynch, E. F. Hutton, and Paine Webber were suffering losses. In the first quarter of 1984, regional firms were earning about 5 percent on equity while the national firms lost money.

The country's big banks ran into trouble not only be expanding their scope of domestic services but also by going international. When they went abroad they began competing in areas in which they were ill equipped. Many of the loans they made were ones local banks had turned down. Losses were enormous.

By late 1984, *The Wall Street Journal* (November 28, 1984) pointed out that "New York's big banks are seeking niches." Many smaller banks had been doing that right along.

In financial service firms, as well as in manufacturing, size and complexity increase unit overheads. According to *Forbes* (September 24, 1984) the ratio of support personnel to salespeople at A. G. Edwards was 1:1. At Merrill Lynch, the figure was close to 3:1. As companies such as American Express continue to become larger and more complicated, they will have more and more trouble competing with smaller firms except in situations in which their gargantuan proportions enable them to provide unique services. Like the dinosaurs, they may outgrow their ability to survive.

## PROFESSIONAL SERVICES

The average size of professional service firms has also increased markedly. The "big eight" auditing firms employ hundreds of accountants and have offices across the United States and around the world. Law firms employing hundreds of attorneys with offices in major cities are becoming common. Some are expanding beyond national boundaries. A number of consulting firms employ hundreds of professionals and have expanded to Europe and Asia. H&R Block helps people prepare tax returns in virtually every American city of any size. Corporations are building chains of walk-in medical and dental service establishments.

In some of these areas, the large, multioffice business fills a need and will prosper. In others, it is simply a manifestation of the widespread obsession with growth and will founder. Managerial vision is needed to tell the difference.

In most areas of medicine, there are obvious benefits to having several physicians associated in a single clinic. To begin with, they can cover for each other to provide continuous availability of medical attention when one of the doctors is away. Sharing facilities, staff, and administrative services provide economies of scale, at least up to the level of several physicians. At some point, and perhaps not very large at that, increasing size and complexity leads to diseconomies of scale. In fact, the typical medical practice has less than two dozen doctors, often fewer than 10.

Many of these small groups are not well managed. Most doctors do not consider themselves business managers, and few are skilled in administration and finance. Their methods are often inefficient. Scheduling is a problem. Getting an appointment may take weeks or even months, and even then patients may have to wait to see the doctor.

This situation has opened the door for health service delivery corporations whose distinctive competence includes good management. They establish offices in convenient locations such as shopping malls. They adopt efficient methods of treatment. They handle scheduling so as to be able to see patients promptly without appointments. They install quality control procedures. They confine themselves to a limited number of standardized procedures for common maladies. In spite of the extra corporate overhead, they are able to offer good service at a competitive price. They appeal to an important segment of the market that values convenience more highly than the continuing personal relationship with a physician in a traditional and sometimes highly inefficient private practice.

A somewhat parallel situation exists in the law. Some firms, usually specializing in a narrow area such as divorce or personal liability, operate much more like a business than like a traditional law firm. They advertise. They provide services standardized for efficiency rather than customized for the needs of the client. They appeal to a segment of the market the usual law office is not well equipped to serve. Many traditional firms consider them to be unethical.

One of these fast-growing firms is Hyatt Legal Services. It handles 20,000 new cases each month. The founder brought legal services at low, standardized rates to many who would have had difficulty affording an attorney in a conventional practice.

Another important factor affecting the practice of law is the growth of the corporate market. Disputes between large corporations can involve hundreds of millions of dollars and can occasion enormous legal fees. Mergers and acquisitions alone have become a major market for legal services. A single transaction can generate eye-popping attorneys' fees.

With the expansion of the corporate market has come the growth of the big-city law firm employing hundreds of attorneys. They are equipped with the latest electronic equipment for researching legal precedents and for creating contracts and other documents covering every imaginable contingency. Not to be outdone by their corporate clients, they occupy lavish quarters in the highest-rent districts. With size, complexity and style have come rapidly escalating overhead structures and often serious management problems. Many large firms struggle with the question of how much of the administration and policysetting should be delegated to professional managers and how much should be retained by the partnership. The collegial relationship among the attorneys adds to the management problem.

The facilities and resources of the large firm represent a distinctive competence to provide superior service to large clients. But many large firms are reluctant to give up other types of work, some of which do not justify the overhead structure. Some of the partners who are not well equipped to contribute in contests between corporate giants are relegated to matters of less moment. Some firms feel that if they do not handle the wills and divorces of their corporate clients, a competitor offering such services will establish a relationship with the client that could lead to loss of corporate business.

Lawyers are subject to the same kind of obsession with growth as manufacturers. But they have still another reason to expand. The partners in a law firm earn money not only on their own work but on that of the firm's associates, or junior members. The ratio of partners to associates is an important determinant of partner's income. Normally, associates expect to become partners within a certain number of years of joining the firm. If the partners are not to suffer a drop in income, they must hire additonal associates not only to replace those who have become partners but to provide associates to work under the new partners. Thus law firms have a built-in incentive to continuing to grow at an accelerating rate.

For these reasons and more, many large firms undertake to handle a very broad range of legal matters, ranging from trivial disputes to major corporate affairs. Lacking managerial vision, they fail to see how such a policy makes them vulnerable to more specialized competitors. There is no way that they can make money dealing with matters in which their costly resources do not provide real value to the client. Yet by continuing to handle these smaller cases, they not only accept unprofitable business but add to the firm's complexity and thus to its overhead burden. This adds to the problem of earning enough on large matters to make the entire operation profitable.

As long as the corporate market was expanding rapidly, most large law firms were able to raise their fees and volume rapidly enough to be highly profitable in spite of uneven strategic management. In recent years, however, the situation has been changing.

Corporations have responded to skyrocketing legal expenses by expanding and upgrading in-house legal departments. More of the routine work is done internally where it does not have to carry the enormous overhead burdens of the large outside firm. Market growth has slowed, and the legal services business has become more competitive. Pressures on large law firms and on the partners within them are mounting. Some have split up. Others are finding it more difficult to maintain their level of income. Like the one-stop financial services emporium, they may be an endangered species.

One beneficiary of the trend toward bigness and scope in law firms has been the specialized partnership. These "boutique" firms build expertise and a reputation in a particular field of specialization. Free from the size and complexity of the larger firm, their unit overheads are lower. But they can still command the high hourly rates of recognized experts in their fields. Because their practices are limited, other firms can refer clients to them without fear that they will exploit the relationship by serving the client in other areas.

A market also seems to be evolving for the very large firm catering to giant corporate clients. It may have a geographical scope paralleling its clients with offices across the country and around the world. It will maintain equipment, facilities, and staff to provide superior services in major corporate matters that would be difficult or impossible for the clients to build internally. It will eschew the handling of matters for which it is ill equipped, such as routine activities, situations not involving a lot of money, and ones requiring unusual specialization.

But the typical large firm trying to be all things to all people will have trouble. Its overhead structure, hiring, promotion, and compensation practices, and firm style and culture simply will not permit being cost-effective over such a wide range of activities. It is inevitably vulnerable to more specialized competitors.

The place of the large, international auditing firm is more secure. True, their rates are higher than small, local firms. But they provide services such as handling complex tax matters, which nearly every sizeable company needs. Small auditing firms cannot afford to maintain such capabilities. Moreover, even a small company often has facilities in several states and countries and needs auditing services in each location. A single auditor must certify the statements of the enterprise. If others check the local books, the certifying firm must then look over their work, which in inefficient and invites friction. Most companies of any size find it more satisfactory to have most or all of the work done by a single, large firm.

But, as in other businesses, the ability to serve one market well leads to the inability to serve others efficiently. The large firms are less cost-effective in serving small businesses than local CPAs. Their overheads are too high. Their methods and attitudes are not attuned to small business. For example, public companies try to show attractive earnings to keep the price of their shares up. Private companies work hard to find methods to report low earnings in order to minimize their taxes. When I established myself as an independent businessman, I quickly found out that the big eight auditor who did an outstanding job for Ventron Corporation was not attuned to my needs. A firm of only a few professional accountants has done a superior job of providing financial advice as well as preparing my tax returns.

Like other businesses, professional service firms need a game plan. They must define their businesses so that they build special capabilities to serve selected market segments. Their plans must deal effectively with the question of growth so that they do not get trapped in a situation in which they are forced to expand beyond a manageable or efficient size. Without effective planning, the tensions, management problems, and split-ups which are already common will become ever more serious.

## WASTE DISPOSAL

The problem of waste disposal has been escalating with the rise in population, in its affluence, and in the dangers inherent in certain types of waste. The dimensions and nature of the waste disposal industry are rapidly changing.

Traditionally, residential waste in cities has been removed by a department of city government. Smaller towns have used services provided by private contractors who also collect commercial and industrial waste. The private firms are usually more efficient. Many middle-sized cities have abandoned municipal waste collection operations in favor of saving money by turning to private contractors to do the job. Large cities have continued to have an arm of government provide the service, partly for political reasons.

Originally, the private waste collectors were primarily small, local firms. Some grew internally. Three corporations grew to substantial size by acquiring many of the smaller local companies. In 1984, one of these was acquired, most of its operations going to one of the other two. At the time of the acquisition, however, the three major firms together accounted for only about 20 percent of the national market.

At the local level there are major economies of scale. Efficiency is dependent on route density, the number of pickups per mile driven. If one company has 50 percent of the customers on a street and two others have 25 percent each, the large firm will enjoy a telling cost advantage.

On a national level, however, there is almost no economy of scale in collecting nonhazardous waste. Trash and garbage cannot be hauled very far. It is inherently a local or small, regional business.

Agglomeration of local companies has provided an opportunity for one important advantage: good management. Many small collection firms have not been well managed. Moreover, many use poor or inappropriate equipment. The larger firms are in a position to develop efficient operating procedures including selection and maintenance of equipment. These represent significant advantages over poorly managed local operations.

As the larger corporations bought smaller ones, their performance in rationalizing the operations of the acquired companies was uneven. One of the large corporations maintained a team for the purpose of quickly changing things in an acquired operation to confrom to standard corporate practice. Another left management and operations largely as they had been. The financial performance of the former was superior.

The kind of operation and equipment that suit one area are less appropriate for others. As a corporation begins standardizing, it begins limiting the area in which it can perform most efficiently. Thus it became increasingly important for these companies to acquire properties that fit the comany's mode of operation. Without economies of scale beyond a standard management approach, willy-nilly acquisitions made no economic sense.

By the mid-1980s, the pattern of development of this industry was becoming clear. Two large corporations were continuing to acquire small firms, especially ones which had been poorly managed and fit their operating methods. Well-managed independents continued to prosper. The third largest firm, which has been slow to adopt a centralized approach to standardizing its operations and acquisitions, had disappeared.

The relative success of the national corporations will depend on how effectively they

1. Develop criteria to guide local operations.
2. Control local operations to exploit the advantages of standardized, rationalized operations (like McDonald's).
3. Leave units with enough flexibility to adjust to their local markets.
4. Learn to market effectively to achieve denser route structures where they are strong.
5. Select acquisitions based on their suitability for their particular type of operation.

The hazardous waste disposal business is quite different. It involves high technology. Regulations are increasingly complex and stringent. Because the cost of safely detoxifying or disposing of hazardous materials is much greater, it can be hauled further. While local firms can still perform simple operations such as neutralizing acids or alkalis, hazardous waste disposal is becoming an increasingly national business based on technical sophistication.

Many of the companies handling solid waste also dispose of hazardous chemicals. Combining the two kinds of operation has only marginal value beyond use of a common corporate name and reputation in marketing. In some cases combining these dissimilar activities has backfired, as when bad publicity about a company in one area harmed it in another. Moreover, to some extent, companies have confused the two businesses and have expected an approach to work in one because it was successful in the other. As in other industries, combining activities increases the size and complexity of the company, causes higher unit overheads. Because these businesses are so different, it is especially difficult to design a corporate culture, style, and approach to be effective in both.

## CAREER PLANNING

In a way, each manager is his own professional service firm. He provides services to his employer and is paid for them.

Many of the principles that apply to developing a corporate game plan also apply to planning a career. A person who develops unique skills that are really needed can name his own price. One who develops more standard capabilities is likely to find himself on a competitive treadmill similar to that of many companies.

The steps an individual takes to build a successful career are parallel to those a company can use. He looks around him at the environment and observes what skills are needed. He takes stock of his own native talents and interests. He observes what others are doing to judge which skills may be in short supply and which may be available in excess. He then "defines his business" in terms of the kind of service he will provide and the capabilities he will develop for long term success. He chooses his education accordingly. He finds employment in an activity in which he can develop his skills and learn from others who are experts in the area. As he builds his ability, he also takes steps to build his reputation.

An important difference between an individual and a company is in adaptability. It is extremely difficult to change what an organization can do well. An individual can often learn to handle a new job more quickly. Thus an individual can change from engineering to marketing to manufacturing, in each area learning skills that will contribute to his ability to be a general manager. However, when an individual is guided primarily by opportunism, and follows a helter-skelter career path, he may suffer from the same fate as many opportunistic companies. He will probably fail to develop the ability to excel at anything.

Companies must maintain a reasonable measure of flexibility. They must also continue to scan their environment for dangers and opportunities. An individual must do the same with his career. Like a company, he develops certain technical skills that have a variety of potential applications. He should apply them where they have high current value *and* where he can further build his unique capabilities.

Individuals who build outstanding capabilities in specialized fields have an excellent opportunity to become rich or famous or both. For example, attorney Joe Flom has realized spectacular success as legal counsel in corporate takeover attempts. Others of my acquaintance have achieved success by building superior skills in bankruptcy law, small business appraisal, health services for professional musicians, and staging business seminars for privately held firms.

The brass ring for the ambitious manager is the job of chief executive officer. It offers a unique combination of financial and personal rewards to individuals who have the interest, ability, and commitment to perform that function.

Before undertaking to prepare himself to be a CEO, a manager should ask himself whether he has the native ability and level of career commitment needed to do that kind of job. A person must not only be reasonably intelligent but must be willing to make tough decisions and to accept responsibility for results. He must not only want the job but must be willing to do whatever is required to succeed within reasonable ethical limits.

A person who has the necessary intellect and character will improve his chances of running a company by acquiring the right training and experience. An MBA degree can be helpful but is not critically important. Experience in several different functions is helpful but not an absolute requirement. Demonstrated ability to handle both line and staff assignments is valuable but not necessary. Demonstrating the ability to make the right things happen, to get things done through other people, is essential.

A mistake made by many talented MBAs with CEO ambitions is to pigeonhole themselves as staff experts. Graduates of the top business schools flock to Wall Street, to large consulting firms, and to positions on the central staffs of large corporations. Such jobs are prestigious and pay handsomely. They take advantage of the skills these people have already developed in analyzing complex business situations and recommending appropriate measures. But they fail to develop either the management skills needed by a line officer of an operating company or the understanding of how top management actions and decisions are translated and distorted as they find their way down to the operating level. Once a person is in such a highly paid prestigious staff career, it often becomes increasingly difficult to get the line experience necessary to qualify to be a CEO.

At this point, I could hardly maintain that management vision is necessary to get a job as a chief executive. The reader has seen that many top executives are seriously lacking in that department. However, boards of directors *try* to find generalists with good objective judgment to run their companies. Hopefully, with the passage of time, vision will become a more important requirement for being selected as a CEO. The person who systematically develops the ability to see both business situations and his own career broadly and objectively will add to his chances of becoming a successful CEO.

## CONCLUSION

As these industries demonstrate, service businesses suffer from the same fundamental problems as manufacturing. Customers (or clients) are different and have different needs. An organization that can serve one market segment particularly well is less able to do a good job for others. Failure to define the business leads to trying to be too many things to too many people. An excessive scope of operations represents vulnerability to competition from more specialized firms. The same maladies—management myopia, obsession with growth and reliance on conventional wisdom—apply in service industries as elsewhere.

Service firms need a good game plan as much as manufacturers do. Their executives have the same need for managerial vision. They need to think in terms of their basic economic function in relation to their environments and to their competitors. They need to identify customers that they can equip themselves to serve better than others can. They need to realize that building resources required to serve one market segment will interfere with their ability to serve others. Without a game plan based on a carefully defined business definition, these firms will find themselves on a competitive treadmill with their future in jeopardy.

# PART 4

# PUTTING THE PLAN TO WORK

# 16

## Making It Happen

A well-chosen game plan is necessary for achieving ambitious goals in business. But planning alone is never enough. Management must make it happen. Companies must build an organized, motivated, and competent team to implement the plan.

Operating methods and techniques, while necessary for effective execution, are beyond the scope of this book. So is the universal need to attract, retain, and motivate superior talent. However, in addition to specific skills, more general corporate characteristics and attitudes also affect a company's ability to implement its plan. A company should systematically develop these general characteristics just as it does the specific capabilities needed to gain superiority in the company's targeted market segments. Investing in building operational skills needs to be part of a strategy.

An essential quality needed to pursue the kind of strategy recommended in this book is the courage to go one's own way. Management must understand the need for the company to define a unique role for itself and to develop capabilities to fill it more effectively than others could. It must be committed to building a distinctive competence. It must find ways to keep its resource development program intact in spite of distractions and adversities.

Such committment derives from the leadership qualities of the chief executive. He must have the vision and character to set a sound course and to persevere. He must help his colleagues see what they can achieve by working single-mindedly to build the particular competence needed to excel in their chosen fields.

A CEO who is easily diverted by each passing opportunity will undermine any game plan. One who focuses on emulating others or conforming to the conventional wisdom will never be able to lead a company in implementing a strategy of being unqiue.

Whether the strength of character needed to lead a company going its own way can be developed is uncertain. However, if a CEO understands how opportunism and following others undermine any efforts to pursue a consistent strategy, he may be able to act more wisely in setting priorities, allocating resources, and sticking to a plan.

Beyond the commitment to a strategy, three characteristics needed to implement it successfully are discipline, flexibility, and creativity. Lack of any of these can subvert management's efforts to execute even the best strategy.

## DISCIPLINE

Discipline is essential to success in business just as it is in athletics, scholarship, or the military. There is no substitute for diligence in either preparation or action. Wishful thinking, on the other hand, is debilitating.

When I became president of Ventron Corporation, it was the world leader in an interesting field of chemistry called metal hydrides. Management hoped that eventually markets would develop for these unusual materials. When they did, the company's ship would come in! Meanwhile, the business was losing over 30 percent on sales. It was investing heavily in a future that might never be. My most important initial task was to instill in management a commitment to live within its means, to produce current earnings *as well as* to build capabilities for the future. As this sense of discipline grew, the company began to prosper and ultimately compiled a record of earnings growth we could all be proud of.

Years later, it was I who needed more discipline. I had proposed to the board a budget with only mediocre earnings. One of the directors opined that a company such as ours should be more profitable. That brought me up short. I knew he was right. I had justified every expense, but the net result was inadequate.

I went back to the drawing board, cut expense levels substantially, and proposed a new budget with higher earnings. It was approved and I tailored our operations to it. Later, looking back on what we had cut, I was able to see that our future had in no way been adversely affected. To the contrary, the company's renewed discipline represented an important competitive strength.

"Investing in the future" is only one form of soft-headedness in management. Bloated administrative staffs are common. Unprofitable products, excessive inventories, and inadequate pricing are other symptoms of lack of discipline. When I joined Ventron, I found that one product had been priced below *variable* costs in order to build volume.

When top management cracks down and demands reductions in staff, product line, or inventories, middle managers scream. "There is no fat here," they complain, "you're asking us to cut out bone." "You're mortgaging the company's future." A central theme of this book is the stategic necessity to develop resources and capabilities for the future. Yet management cannot afford to lose sight of the present. Fiscal control is itself a key capability needed for future success.

Instilling discipline is not easy. Years ago, the managment of a large plumbing supply manufacturer was killed in an airplane crash. Even before the tragedy, the company's performance had been only so-so. The board brought in a new CEO with impressive credentials to set the company on a new course. While he improved operations in a number of areas, financial performance continued to lag.

Then an aggressive entrepreneur gained control of the company and installed himself as CEO. Instead of a scalpel, he used an axe. On day one, he cut the corporate staff by 50 percent. Some good people were dismissed. The old management thought he had destroyed the company. Indeed, he had made some errors in detail. But his dramatic move produced results that the professional manager had been unable to achieve. Earnings improved not only in the short term but over time. Fifteen years later, the company was still regularly returning over 20 percent on equity. The discipline instilled by the new boss was what the company had needed.

Japanese companies systematically target executive productivity as an area for improvement just as they do manufacturing efficiency. Some methodically hold the number of executives constant as they expand. Others that are are not growing hire fewer executives each year than the number retiring.

As with individuals, one of the greatest threats to corporate discipline is success. When pioneering companies such as Polaroid and Xerox become successful, they tend to spend without restraint. Unusual employee benefits, indulgent personnel policies, generous charitable contributions, and extensive public service activities become part of the corporate culture. Later, it is difficult to adjust to the hard realities of a more competitive world. No doubt the success of Ventron, as well as the vestiges of its former free-spending culture, contributed to the soft-headed budget noted above.

Discipline applies not only to spending. Management needs discipline to maintain product quality, dedication to customer service, safety in operations, and, in fact, the integrity of the enterprise. Discipline is necesary for the performance in every function, from accounting to research. It was Steven Jobs' unbending insistence on achieving the product features he envisioned that differentiated Apple Computer from its early competitors. Nearly every successful executive is characterized by total commitment to his goals and by the self-discipline needed to achieve them.

## FLEXIBILITY

Flexibility sounds like the antithesis of discipline. Unseeing discipline can indeed lead to a dangerous rigidity. Yet both of these qualities are important. In fact, discipline is sometimes needed to maintain flexibility.

For example, finance is an area in which flexibility is essential. Yet companies often fail to maintain enough financial flexibility to remain solvent when they meet adversity. Because debt is cheaper than equity, borrowing heavily to finance growth is always tempting. But sound management requires the discipline to maintain adequate financial flexibility. The business battlefield is littered with the corpses of firms that yielded to the temptation to burden the balance sheet with excessive debt.

Flexibility is not free. Montgomery Ward, the giant retail chain, demonstrated how expensive financial flexibility can be. After World War II, its chairman refused to commit the money needed to keep operations competitive. He feared a repeat of the Great Depression and put financial flexibility ahead of all other considerations. He amassed a cash hoard amounting to 90 percent of net worth, while allowing his organization and facilities to deteriorate badly. When new management was brought in, it invested the company's money in rebuilding the organization and physical plant. But Montgomery Ward had ben so weakened that it never fully recovered. For decades, first as an independent entity and later as a Mobil subsidiary, Montgomery Ward's results have been poor.

The balance a company strikes between flexibility and commitment has a powerful influence not just on its progress, but on whether it survives at all.

Excessive rigidity is a danger in any phase of business. His initial success with mass production has led Henry Ford to a pig-headed fixation on absolute standardization. This in turn led to the loss of industry leadership to GM. More recently the insistence of American auto manufacturers on giving consumers an almost infinite choice of options is costing them dearly. The Japanese seem to have found a better compromise between standardization and variety. In 1984, Honda offered a total of 32 varieties of its popular Accord model, while the Ford Thunderbird came in 69,000 varieties and the Chevrolet Citation in more than 32,000. The extra cost required to giving buyers such a wide choice was estimated at $800–$1200 per automobile.

Times change. A fixation on any single technology, marketing approach, or manufacturing technique can lead to disaster. Companies must respond to changes in the world in which they operate.

At the same time, success requires commitment. Leadership, whether in technology, manufacturing skills, or marketing enterprise, usually takes years of investing in building capability. Success requires the vision to balance commitment to a unique approach with willingness to change. It requires the character to impose the discipline needed for effectiveness without adopting the rigidity that insures eventual failure.

As management formulates its resource development plan, it must strike another kind of balance. The plan must be sufficiently specific to yield genuine competitive advantages in the targeted market segments. Yet the capabilities the company develops must be sufficiently general and flexible that a small change in the environment will not render them obsolete.

As a business pursues its strategy, it must carefully monitor its progress. If things do not go as planned, management must ask itself why. Has it chosen the wrong strategy? Has its implementation been inept? Or did it misjudge the difficulty of what it undertook and set unrealistic goals? To succeed, a company must be able to persevere even in the face of discouraging results. It must at the same time be sufficiently flexible to be able to modify the game plan when it is clear that its strategy is flawed.

## CREATIVITY

In business, creativity leads to innovation, employing new and better ways to serve customers. People often associate innovation in business with the physical sciences; incorporating new technology in new products or processes. Actually, creativity can contribute to any phase of business, from distribution to accounting. McDonald's was creative, as was the introduction of self-service supermarkets and discount retailing.

Creativity depends on the state of mind of a person or of an organization. If one looks, chances are one will see. If one's mind is open and if he seeks new and better ways, he can find them. But if one's thinking is chained to the status quo, limited by unstated assumptions reflecting existing methods and habits, one will not be able to innovate.

Years ago, Joseph Juran revealed important insights about corporate creativity in his book *Managerial Breakthrough and Control* (McGraw-Hill, 1964). New companies and new industries are born, he wrote, as the result of innovation. Once the new ways of doing things are established, competition prompts companies to refine methods, focusing on efficiency. As the companies grow, they use more division of labor, more specialists to continue to wring pennies or even fractions of a cent out of costs. As this procedure continues, companies become more rigid, more systematized, less able to innovate.

Ultimately, the environment changes. New technology becomes available. Customers have new needs. The situation calls for innovation. But the big, old companies have trouble responding. The specialists in every part of the industry leaders have a vested interest in the status quo. Their value is in their ability to operate efficiently based on the old technology, the old needs of the market, the established way of doing business.

This clash of the need for innovation and the inertia of the bureaucracy can have either of two results. The established company can renew itself by going through wrenching change. This seldom happens before earnings drop and the company's continuing existence is threatened. Often a new top management and extensive executive turnover are required to achieve the changes needed for survival. The alternative is decline and often complete failure.

In the cash register business, for example, NCR was the dominant factor until electronics came along. Slow to give up its traditional approaches, it lost a major part of the market to upstart companies such as Data Terminal Systems that quickly seized on the opportunity opened by electronics technology. Ultimately, however, NCR adopted the new technology and achieved a resurgence in growth and profitability.

In other changing industries, the leaders have been unable to adapt. Baldwin Locomotive fell to the diesel engine. The old-fashioned hamburger heavens lost out to McDonald's. Big Steel has not responded effectively to either the large foreign mills nor to the domestic minimills and continues to ail. The American automobile industry is struggling to responding to changing market and competitive patterns. General Motors' Saturn program to revolutionize small car manufacture was born of years of inability to match Japanese productivity.

Innovation requires understanding what people will buy. One of the most common business mistakes is introducing a wonderful, new product or service no one wants or needs. At the same time, significant innovation usually involves products or services not previously available. Often, the customers themselves would not have been able to predict the extent to which they would buy the new item.

Successful innovation is more often based on insight and intuition than on systematic market research. Eastman Kodak was far better qualified to introduce instant photography than was Polaroid. But it didn't believe that the market would accept the poor quality of the early instant snapshots. Dr. Land was sufficiently convinced of the marketability of his product that he bet his company on its immediate success. And, of course, we now know that he was right.

In discussing the potential for a new technology, Nobel laureate Herbert C. Brown once observed, "Market research is useless. It will only reveal one of two things. One is that a similar product or technology already exists, so that it is too late to innovate. The other is that since no one is using it, no market exists. In either case, market research will lead to a conclusion against innovation." Successful innovation depends much more on vision and imagination than on systematic managerial techniques, valuable as the latter may be.

To innovate, a company must be able to see what people need and want. It must also be able to see how its organization thinks and reacts to new challenges and opportunities. Wise management with vision can build an organization capable of adjusting to a changing environment and, in fact, of being an agent of change itself. Companies such as IBM, 3M, and General Electric have developed the corporate character needed to renew themselves continually, to adapt, to seize on new technologies, and to remain healthy despite their size and their vested interests in the status quo. Unless a company can develop a climate that fosters innovation, it risks going the way of the steam locomotive manufacturers or of the steel industry.

## REWARDS

Executives who successfully implement a sound strategy and game plan based on a unique definition can reap rich rewards. They are among the best paid members of the community. Their achievements are recognized not only by their colleagues in their companies but in the business community and beyond. Outstanding achievement brings additional leadership opportunities not only in business but in other roles in society. Perhaps the most important reward is the satisfaction of knowing that one has contributed to the well-being of many people.

Effective executives create jobs. They provide opportunities for their subordinates to grow and to gain satisfaction from their own work. They give their customers a more attractive choice. They add to the wealth of their shareholders. As they build their companies' competence to do a better job for their customers, they are at the same time adding to the economic capability of the nation. They are playing an important role in enhancing the quality of life. The sense of achievement derived from knowing one has made that kind of contribution is quite special.

Being an executive involves taking risks. But when one thinks deeply about the situation, he sees that the risks in varioius courses of action are not what they seem to be. The "safe" course of diversifying may be more risky than focusing on a narrower area in which one is better qualified. The "safe" course of following the conventional wisdom is fraught with danger. The "safe" course of emulating successful companies may limit only the upside possibilities not the downside exposure.

Our changing world provides a wealth of business opportunities. As Apple Computer, Toys "R" Us, Nucor, and hundreds of others continue to demonstrate, companies now can be more successful more quickly than ever before. One company, Compaq Computer has even sold more than $100 million in its first full year of operation.

What is required is not new. Executives must see where their particular opportunities lie. They must have the courage to go their own way, to commit to building a unique competence to serving the specific customer groups they have selected. They must define their businesses, formulate sound strategies, and follow a game plan designed for their own unique situations. Then they must make it happen. For those executives who can perform this kind of leadership, the rewards are unlimited.

# Index